Early American Costume

An
Early
American
Society
Book

The editors of *Early American Life*, the Society's official magazine, have checked this book for historical and, where possible, factual accuracy. Opinions and interpretations expressed within its pages have been left as written by the author. It is the objective of the Society to sponsor and recommend books that it feels have lasting value to persons interested in colonial and early American times—books that are both entertaining and enlightening.

Robert G. Miner
President and Editor of Publications

Early American Costume

Estelle Ansley Worrell

Stackpole Books

EARLY AMERICAN COSTUME

Published by
STACKPOLE BOOKS
Cameron and Kelker Streets
Harrisburg, Pa. 17105

391
W

Printed in the U.S.A.

Library of Congress Cataloging in Publication Data

Worrell, Estelle Ansley, 1929-
  Early American costume.

  1. Costume—United States—History. I. Title.
GT607.W67   391′.00973   75-17906
ISBN 0-8117-0539-0

Contents

"It is impossible to know who is noble, who is worshipful, who is a gentleman, and who is not because all persons dress indiscriminantly in silks, velvets, and satens, damaskes, and taffeties, and suche like, not withstanding that they be both base by birthe, meane by estate, and servile by calling. I count this a great confusion, and a general disorder: God be merciful unto us." So complained the English Puritan Philip Stubbes in his *Anatomie of Abuses* published in England in 1583.

Not only was it difficult then to tell what or who a person was by his clothes, but in the coming years it would be even more difficult.

Sumptuary laws to define what people might or might not wear were passed again and again in England and America, only to be repealed or simply ignored. With the first attempts to settle America the seeds of independence were already in the minds of the people, particularly in the minds of the English.

CHAPTER 1

Designing for Theatre

WHEN THE DRAMA, the humor, or the music stimulates the emotions and the ears of the audience, it should be complemented by something to stimulate the eyes as well. The movement of the actors, the sets, and the costumes all stimulate and please the audience visually. By capturing one more of the senses of each member of the audience we involve him in one more way. The more of his senses he uses the more he will participate psychologically in the performance.

Designers in today's visual world have a challenge that designers in the past did not have: Our audiences expect, and demand, more because they are accustomed to more. We live in a world of color television, beautifully illustrated books, lavish movies and stage productions, and brilliant, expensive advertising in our homes, stores, on the streets—everywhere. Stage and costume design has to be good in order to compete with all that. Audience involvement is as important as the performance. The ability of the cast and the designers to bring out that involvement is what makes a great performance great!

A COSTUME SHOULD EXPRESS THE MOOD AND SPIRIT OF THE TIMES

Since this book is one about American historical clothing, then I must assume that you, the designer, are primarily concerned with a dramatization set, at least in part, in America before 1850. In order to do this well you must know something about the times which are being dramatized. In my history descriptions accompanying the drawings, I have tried to give you a feeling for the times and for the kind of person who might have worn those clothes as well as facts directly concerned with them. A good designer will impart something of the times, an attitude, or the spirit of the times into his designs as well as facts. It is an intangible something that you will feel if you become involved in and enthusiastic about your work.

The spirit of the times can be shown in one way by the manner of wearing or fastening the clothes as well as in the design of them. The manner of wearing or even holding a shawl, buttoning a coat, tying a cravat, draping a skirt, or shaping a hat brim is as important to a period as the clothes themselves. The drawings always show the fashionable manner of wearing that particular article of clothing. The old saying, "It's the little things that count," can be applied to designing costumes. With few exceptions in history, costume has changed gradually. Even when things appear to have come about spontaneously, on closer study there are signs to be found which were predicting the change.

I have organized the costume drawings by decade. Within each group the men are arranged with the fashionable clothes first, the working clothes next, and then the military. Women's clothes follow those of the men. Children's clothes, with the older ones first, then the younger ones and babies, are at the end. Not every group has all types of clothes or all age groups because it depends on the historical material available and what was going on during that period.

Indians The exception to this order of arranging the costumes are the Indians; they appear in four of the groups and are placed at the beginning of the decade. Although their dress changed little over a long period of time they are placed as they are because that is the time in which they were most directly involved with our history. They are grouped according to racial and language stock based on the United States Government classification given in most encyclopedias. It would take a whole volume in order to give costumes by tribe but the groups with the same anthropological background dressed in much the same fashion since they were related.

When working with Indians of a particular area of the United States there might be some degree of overlapping as to climate. For instance, the tribes farthest south of the Algonkian group might dress somewhat like the Muskhogean groups while the northernmost tribes of the Muskhogeans might wear certain items like the northern tribes. This would be true of certain borderline tribes where you might take more liberties in combining costumes.

One rule to remember is that as the Indian came in closer contact with the white man he tended to dress more like him. While the white man was adopting Indian clothes, the Indian was adopting shirts and trousers to cover his nudity, which shocked the white man.

Wherever the two cultures were in close contact they had a tendency to look more like each other as demonstrated in Figures 145 and 160. Several early 19th century portraits of Indian chiefs show them dressed in the same manner as these two Indian agents.

Attitudes Sometimes you may have to take small liberties with history because certain things have, through the years, become associated with certain attitudes. For instance, it is difficult to make a serious hero out of Figure 50 because the dandy is more likely to provoke laughter from the audience. But don't be afraid to attempt it if you and the director feel you can accomplish it. It depends on the statement you are trying to make and the times in which you are trying to make it. There are no set rules because theatre deals with people whose ideals constantly change and every costume must be considered individually in the time in which it is designed as well as the times it represents.

What is ridiculous or immoral in one decade will not necessarily be so in another decade. What is bright in one era may be considered somber in another. Even an old woman of 1810 would, for instance, wear lighter, brighter colors than a young person of the 1840s. Originally calico was imported from India and was so cheap that only poor people wore it during the 18th century. By 1830 it had become so fashionable that all women were wearing it; calico, like many things, means one thing during one period and something quite different in another.

Mix and Match One might ask, "Why should I have to design my own when the drawings show what was worn in every decade in America up until 1850?" Well, aside from the fact of characterization there is another more practical reason—a play may have only two or three characters but many have twenty or thirty and historical pageants sometimes have even more. When you have so many characters are you going to dress them all exactly the same?

I've given the coats, riding habits, dressing gowns, and aprons to help you create costumes for any special need but even that may not be enough for a large cast.

When working within a decade you should feel free to mix and match the different parts of the costumes that have similar lines. You can use a sleeve or collar from one dress and the bodice or skirt of another. Some of the costume drawings are composites in instances where a great deal of historical material was available. When there were many dresses of similar design I used two or three composites in order to give as accurate a picture of the times as possible without doing so many plates of similar design.

America had a great variety of styles up until recent years because there were people in every colony and even in frontier areas who could and did afford the very latest fashions. But as a rule, except for the well-to-do fashionable people, most people in frontier areas would wear clothes of, say, the decade before because of the difficulty of acquiring new styles.

Clothes were kept until they were quite worn, then often bequeathed to family or friends in the event of the owner's death. By the time slaves or servants or very poor people received them they might be two or even three decades old. I did find some American portraits which show people wearing clothes that had been the current fashion in Europe as much as twenty-five, and in a few cases of older people, fifty, years earlier.

Once you know these historical facts, then it becomes a matter of characterization. What kind of people would wear the latest styles? The answer might be: the rich; the recently arrived middle class or well-to-do immigrants; the families of merchants, sea captains, or governors; and other people who might have had recent contact with Europe. But any one of these people might also be extremely conservative and you have the question of age and personality to consider, so you can see that the proper historic period is only the beginning.

Research For readers who will be doing research other than in this book you may sometimes have to disregard the dates on historical portraits and paintings. Historians take into consideration, first of all, the dates when the painter (if he is known) lived. Then they consider the years during which he was believed to have painted. They base the dating on the way in which the painter signed his work, on his painting style, where he lived or traveled at certain times in his life and so on. They are more likely to date paintings too early than too late.

One dress in a large museum has a different date in each of three publications in which it appears. I wrote to the museum to try to find the accurate date. The museum dates it only as "late 18th century" so each author had given the date which his research showed it to be. In one other case two different books showed the same portrait dated with a difference of fifty years! Since one of the books had been published thirty years before the other, one might assume that the later of the two authors used material that had not been available when the first one wrote his book.

Designing for Theatre

The Language of Clothes   Clothes tell us a great deal about a person as an individual but they tell us more than that. Immediately upon seeing a person we can often tell where he has been or is going, whether he is well or ill, what the weather is at the moment, his mode of travel, and whether he is working or relaxing, because clothes have a language all their own.

Throughout my history drawings I have shown cloaks or coats, aprons, dressing gowns, and working clothes as well as fashionable clothing. Each of these in its own way makes a statement when worn by a character in a play (or in real life as well).

Coats and Cloaks   The most obvious symbol in the language of clothes is the coat or cloak. When an actor makes an entrance wearing a cloak, you know before any dialogue is spoken that he has been out-of-doors (most likely), has been traveling; that it is cold, or that he is leaving. The cloak gives you the visual message before words are spoken.

A long journey can be suggested by the creative use of a coat without having to build an expensive set. The coat can be put on at the end of a scene, and when it is worn when the actor makes his re-entry later in the play, you assume that he has been traveling in the meantime.

In one play I designed at Nashville Children's Theatre we had to show a journey of several weeks from Boston to Alabama during the 19th century. During the first scene the actress was helped into her coat on stage with her bonnet and her gloves. She was trim and neat and attractive as she picked up her wicker suitcase with leather straps around it. In the next scene she arrived in Alabama in the heat of late spring wearing the same outfit. Immediately the audience understood that she had been traveling and that time had passed—there was little need for explanation.

We went one step further, though, because we had to show that she had had a hot, miserable, and seemingly endless trip. When she knocked on the door and was welcomed into the house (a new set), her hat was crooked, her hair falling down, her coat unbuttoned, and her wicker suitcase had a broken strap. When the servant took her coat she shook out the dust (talcum powder) and the hot, sticky, dusty trip seemed believably real. The costume designer and the director had created a journey almost entirely by the use of costume.

Aside from travel, coats or cloaks can symbolize the climate, the weather, or the changing of the seasons.

A cloak can make a prediction, too, such as when the actor either picks up his coat or hat or begins putting it on. Even before he announces verbally that he is leaving he has already announced it visually.

And, after Macintosh invented his raincoat in the early 19th century, a raincoat on an actor could tell you something in particular about the weather.

Riding Habits   After the Revolution riding habits became extremely fashionable but you can create a riding habit in any period by understanding a few facts about them.

Women's riding clothes always imitated the current fashionable doublet or coat worn by gentlemen of the same period. Use the skirt with a feminine version of the doublet and also the fashionable man's hat. To get an idea of how riding habits for women looked you might start by examining the clothes of little boys who are still in skirts such as Figures 12, 33, 47, and 122. After 1770 you can still find inspiration in little boys' jackets and blouses to be worn with the current skirts such as Figures 138, 183, 198, and 212. Little boys' clothes always imitated their mothers' fashions as much as their fathers' and in some periods even more so.

Men's hats were always worn with feminine habits but whether a top hat or a tricorne, it was always decorated with plumes and cocked much more dramatically than when worn by men. In almost all periods women's riding hats were worn at the front of the head with the brim up in back and the plumes in back.

Riding habits serve much the same purpose as coats and capes but their use increases your possibilities of design. A riding jacket and hat can be designed to coordinate with the skirt of a dress already worn by the same character. This will save money and facilitate the costume change at the same time.

Dressing Gowns   Dressing gowns are a very useful symbol in the theatre for establishing a mood of informality, intimacy, illness, time of morning or night, pregnancy, etc. The full flowing robes are particularly attractive on overweight women.

These gowns make possible a simple and quick costume change since they are usually worn over parts of other costumes such as petticoats, corsets, breeches, shirts, vests, or skirts. In most cases only the coat or bodice needs to be removed. In some instances when there isn't time for a change the loose dressing gown can be quickly put on over a complete costume and then removed just as quickly.

Sometimes dressing gowns can serve as a bridge between two costumes as when only a part of a costume is worn with a dressing gown, then the gown removed and the rest of the costume added.

Aprons   Aprons for both men and women usually symbolize work of some sort; for children, usually play or just protection of good clothes. But during the 18th century aprons were worn for fashion also.

The boy's apron in Figure 109 was also worn by adults. One old print of an English barber shows him wearing a plain white one in the identical shape.

Women appear wearing the apron of Figure 108. The more beautiful the apron, the less likely that it was worn for working other than for doing needlework. Some aprons were lacy, satin, or beautifully embroidered, and sometimes all three at once as in Figure 133, which is definitely not a work apron. The aprons of Figures 78 and 79 are part of the fashionable costume rather than for working although aprons were used for work during that period.

An apron is a very inexpensive costume change but it should never be treated carelessly because the apron style is as important for creating the feel of the period as the clothes worn under it.

Poverty or Servitude   To show poverty or some form of servitude, eliminate any decorations from the designs of the period because expensive lace, buttons, ribbons, etc., were treasured items which could be removed from old clothes and used again on new ones. A costume, then, might be literally stripped of any decoration that was not actually a part of it, such as embroidery, before being handed down to less fortunate individuals.

In cases where a person of low means preferred to make his or her own clothes, they would be made of coarser, less expensive fabrics than those handed down.

Servants and slaves of very wealthy families would have dressed better than many free men who suffered extremely hard times. The costume of Figure 146 is a good example since one portrait shows both George Washington and his favorite servant wearing clothes of almost identical cut. In general, the richer the family, the more expensively the servants were dressed. There are individual cases where the opposite is true as with a "Simon Legree" type of master but that is more a matter of characterization than of authenticity.

A COSTUME SHOULD TELL SOMETHING ABOUT THE CHARACTER

Authenticity is only part of the requirements for well-designed costumes. The very moment a character makes his entrance his costume can make a statement about him. It can tell obvious or external things such as that he is young or old, rich or poor, fashionable or conservative, and so on.

What of the more subtle things such as intelligence, generosity, honesty, confidence, and all those things which are less obvious or internal? They are, of course, more difficult to convey for the beginning designer.

When considering both the external, or obvious, and the internal or less obvious characteristics, the challenge is even greater. For instance, a character might be honest, intelligent, and rich—or honest, intelligent, but poor.

It is a strange situation, but often the most professionally designed costumes receive the fewest comments and sometimes the worst ones bring many compliments such as, "The costumes are so pretty!"

Costumes, when well designed, become a part of the character and are so natural that the audience takes them for granted. (This is true only of some audiences, because any professional designer or critic would recognize the quality.) When they are so obviously "costumes," they will receive many comments because they are separate from the character; in other words, they are make-believe clothes on actors merely playing a part. This is true of the quality of acting also. Every actor knows that a part can be played so convincingly, so naturally, that the audience really believes he is that person. When he plays the part so that you can't forget he is an actor, then he has really not been a good actor. The clothes and the actor should melt together and become an individual who you can believe is living at that moment.

For showing generosity and openness, the character's clothing can complement his outward attitudes with an open coat and a relaxed fit (don't confuse *relaxed* with *loose*) along with a hat tilted just slightly toward the back.

To indicate inward attitude, a coat might fit tightly and be buttoned up all the way. The hat brim might be pulled down over the face. Don't cock the hat, just bend the brim down.

A feeling of sharpness, hardness, or evil can be emphasized by incorporating as many points in your design as possible within the period, such as exaggerated lapels, coattails, or vest points. The shoes can have pointed toes and the hat a stiff rather than soft plume.

To show amiable or good qualities you might use more curves. All these things can be used in a very subtle way or they can be exaggerated in a burlesque fashion depending on the character.

Make sure that any use of these symbols is intentional because any piece of clothing that won't stay in place can give an unstable feeling to your character. It has on many occasions unintentionally turned a hero into a clown.

Hoops   A swinging hoop can be ridiculous if it is too large, if the hoop is too low or too high, or if it is worn without petticoats over it. Hoops and farthingales have been used in burlesque for centuries with hilarious results with or without the proper undergarments. When you use the hoop in a serious drama, be sure you use it skillfully.

Hats   Perhaps it is because they are so close to our faces that hats, and the way they are worn, tell so much about us. It was said in the early West that one cowboy could tell where another one was from by the way his hat was creased, rolled, cocked, and worn.

Every soldier or sailor since the earliest colony has known that hats have their own language. It's incredible that every man in a regiment can follow regulations and still at the same time wear his hat in such an individual way. Hats follow styles but what one does to his and the way he wears it make it "one-of-a-kind."

One of the most expressive articles of clothing in American history was the cloth bonnet of the late 18th and early 19th century. It can be demure, evil, ridiculous, beautiful, hilarious, or almost anything you want in either drama or comedy by its size, shape, and manner of wearing.

Any hat in any period can be used to express character, not only by the way it is worn but by the way an actor treats it. A 17th century Cavalier can use it to bow with, wave under his arm and so on. The very manner of pushing a hat back or pulling it down in front can make a statement as well as the way it is put on, removed, carried, or thrown.

The decoration on the hat or bonnet can be another language in itself, such as curled ribbons that bob up and down or a loose plume that flops back and forth.

The fit of a hat can also be a means of expression as when a hat is too large and comes too far down on the head, or too small and sits up on top. A poorly fitting hat might fall forward or even fall off each time an actor bends over. Just make sure that all these things are *intentional* lest they have the opposite effect on your audience.

Color   Various symbols have been attached to colors through the centuries and they persist even today. You may or may not want to use them. In Christian art blue has symbolized goodness. It has for hundreds of years been used for the robes of the Virgin Mary. White has always symbolized Christ or purity. Purple was so symbolic of royalty that in some countries the law forbade commoners to wear it.

There are the old associations that have been handed down like "green with envy," "in a blue mood," "black with despair," or "yellow coward." Each astrological sign has a symbolic color which you might refer to for association with certain personality traits. This can become tiresome if carried too far, I think, but it can be of some help if you are designing for the first time by giving you something to start with.

Be a little careful with the color yellow, though, for it can symbolize cowardliness or a sunny, happy disposition. It also is the color assigned to the Gemini sign.

Designers often use basic color families for grouping characters of similar motives or personalities, such as warm colors for the "good guys" and cool, grayed colors for the "bad guys." In a play concerning the Revolution this system of color families might help the audience to keep the Tories separate from the Whigs. Perhaps, since the British soldiers wore red coats, all the loyalist ladies could wear dresses in the red family from pinks to maroons, rusts, orange, etc., in subtle or bright hues. On the other hand, since green is the complement of red, they might all wear shades of green.

When one character grows through more than one stage of life during the story, he or she might wear the same color all the way through but in different shades. A woman might, for instance, start out in pink, then wear bright red, orange, and finally soft rose or maroon in later years.

Psychological as well as chronological age can be treated in this manner when a character matures or blossoms through insight or experience. It can be used in the opposite way, too, as a character regresses or withdraws.

It is important that the costume designer confer with the set designer as to color. At Nashville Children's Theatre we usually are told by the director in the beginning whether he sees a new play as a costume show or a scenery show. This way one of the two designers then sets the mood and the other complements it.

Certain lights and scenery colors will wash out some of the costume colors if this dominance is not agreed upon beforehand.

The tone or intensity of a color can be as important as the color itself. The tone can set a mood for a whole scene or even the whole play. It can even represent a period in history such as the somber colors of the 1840s or the whites and bright hues at the beginning of the 1800s.

Tone was used most effectively in the old black-and-white movies and early television since photography is an abstract design of grays. It forced the designers to think in terms of tone rather than color. After you have selected your color schemes, analyze the tones as if you were doing them for a black-and-white movie and you may change some to deeper or softer tones and tints.

Texture   Coarsely woven fabrics usually symbolize poverty, or in more recent years, work clothes and sportswear. But the weave must be exaggerated on stage in order to be noticed.

A subtle sheen is more elegant and expensive looking than a hard shine. If you want satin, use only good quality satin or *peau-de-soie*. If you can't afford these, then use inexpensive taffeta or one of the many new synthetics that are not too shiny for a look of quality. A cheap satin comes off as just that—cheap satin—on stage. It is great for ladies of questionable character or for a comic or "bad" character. This is one of the most common mistakes of inexperienced costumers who think of satin as "rich" or "elegant" only to discover too late that just the opposite is true on stage.

Form   The form or silhouette of every character must be considered in relation to the character and to the individual actor playing the part. For comedy, it is easy to exaggerate a skirt length or fullness or perhaps a sleeve or shoulders. In drama these things must be done very carefully. A hero's shoulders might be padded, but only so they look natural—not exaggerated as in comedy. An old man's stomach or a dowager's bosom might be padded but, again, in drama it should be subtle and natural. Padding is a necessity in theatre because casting a person who has the ability and experience to do a role well is the first consideration but he may not be exactly the right physical type as well. I have found the best way to pad is first to make a snugly fitting vest or body and then sew all the padding to that. Then there is no slipping; it will become a part of the actor's body and move with him. Foam rubber is easy to obtain and makes a lightweight padding. I always cover the padding on the outside, encasing the foam in between the cover and vest. These padded stomachs, bosoms, shoulders, backs, etc., can be used again if they are stored away after the run of the play.

It helps to know a little about what happens to the human form as it ages. The youthful high bosom or chest will move down while the waistline moves up until in advanced age they almost meet. The neck gets shorter and the head goes forward as the back becomes more rounded. From the front the appearance is broad in the middle at the waist and narrow in the shoulders because of the sloping or drooping.

This can be taken to any degree with padding and posture, depending on how much you need to age the character. It can also be used to make, say, an older actress have a more youthful silhouette by raising her bustline, cinching in her waist, getting the chin up by design or posture.

Human Nature   There must be consistency in portraying character. There are certain things that people won't do or can always be expected to do. Some women, for instance, just won't (absolutely) expose too much of the breasts while other women can't be expected to hide very much.

Situation comedies and dramatic series on television which use the same characters week after week adhere to this strictly. There are certain traits and rules of behavior that are consistent with each character. Opportunities for great laughs or dramatic moments are sometimes passed up because they would not suit the character. Problems must always be solved within the limitations of the character's morals, prejudices, intelligence, and so forth.

On the other hand, a dress of a different character type may be used to point up a dramatic change in character or attitude or to reveal real but formerly suppressed attitudes.

In designing for old characters, remember that old people often cling to all or parts of the clothing that was fashionable in earlier years. Many famous statesmen, Benjamin Franklin for one, continued to wear knee breeches or full coats for many years after young fashion-conscious gentlemen adopted trousers or pantaloons and cutaway coats.

Today we have many different kinds of clothing: formal, cocktail, daytime, sports (tennis, skiing, horseback riding, car riding, etc.). In the past women, and men too, had to adapt the same dress or coat to serve many purposes.

The more you observe people around you—young, old, outgoing or shy—the better designer you will become. The best way to understand people is to be open to them, to like them, and listen to them. Note that although old or conservative persons cling to former fashions, they never, except in the case of eccentrics, retain *all* of the old styles. They will adopt a new style hat, kerchief, or cravat, etc. They almost invariably express some acceptance of the new in their costume. This can be used as a matter of degree in character expression: The more youthful and outgoing an old person is, the more elements in his costume will be contemporary. This has often been demonstrated in comedy by the "swinging grandmother" who dresses like a teen-ager and drives a sports car or rides a motorcycle. It can also be done in serious drama in a less obvious manner.

The Physical Side of Design   The physical assets or flaws of the actor must be considered. For example, suppose your hero should wear the hose and stockings of Figures 2 and 3. He is the best actor for the part, he has good shoulders, is a great actor, with a handsome face, but, alas, has legs which would be certain to provoke laughter when he walked on stage.

You may then want, for everyone's sake, to put him in the long hose or cannions of Figures 4 or 14 or hide his legs under the robe of Figure 27 or pantaloons of Figure 6. In other words, take a few liberties with history for the sake of drama. The more you understand history, the more successfully you can do this.

Don't fail to take into consideration that actors are sensitive about their measurements and figure flaws, while at the same time particularly eager to display their assets. A successful costume is designed first for the character, the make-believe person, but it must also be made for the real person—the actor.

One old rule among costume designers is, "Never ask an actor what his or her measurements are." You must always measure him or her yourself. Even having someone else measure for you can lead to disaster because only the person who does the measuring knows how tightly the tape was held or just how much was allowed for the clothes the actor was wearing at the time, etc. Only the person who actually does the measuring knows if the actress was "sucking in" her waistline or pushing out the

bosom, those things that one can sense. The person who will do the sewing should be the one to do the measuring, whenever possible.

The Actor's Cooperation   The actor needs to understand the costumes of the period but unfortunately actors as well as directors do not always make the effort to do so.

Any actor who really wants to perform to the best of his ability will naturally want to know something about the costumes of the period he is dramatizing. Certain mannerisms and customs are associated with each style. I have suggested, in each figure, the stance or attitude associated with the wearing of that costume although I was limited somewhat by the primary objective of showing the costumes clearly and simply. In Figure 132, for instance, the fashionable posture taught to any young lady was "Keep the elbows back and chin forward and up." This was not only fashionable, but was a necessity because of the large panniers or side hoops.

The large padded and stuffed sleeves of Figure 31 required the arms to be held out away from the body as did the sleeves again in the 1830s when large stuffed sleeves returned to fashion.

The stance of the soldiers in Figure 75 was a matter of necessity. Because of the wide-topped boots the men had to "walk wide." The gentleman of Figure 93 has his hand in his waistcoat because it was stylish to wear it only partly buttoned to let ventilation in. It made a natural, tempting sling for one's arm.

A really good actor will study body language and costume so that his every movement will complement his character and the character of the historical period.

It is possible for the designer to force a certain amount of the proper posture and attitude. A dress like that of Figure 132 can be made so narrow across the bodice back that the actress will have to keep her elbows back. A dress or coat can be heavily weighted with drapery or fishing weights to force a train to pull or a sleeve to hang correctly. And of course a real busk can be used in a bodice front to give the proper rigidity to it. This must be done in a spirit of cooperation between the designer, director, and actor. For this reason, it should be looked upon as a way of helping the actor attain the proper look rather than as a sneaky way of forcing it.

It will be of some help in the very beginning if you draw your costume plate with the correct stance so that the director and actors can visually associate the period, the costume, the stance of the period, and the attitude of that particular character.

Don't worry about wrinkled tights—the old stockings always wrinkled, even bagged. Clothes were stretched at the elbows and knees too.

Sleeves were cut so that the seams were in the front and back in the shape of the arm. When the arm is held straight down at the side, the elbows will bag in back. But remember that with very full skirts and sleeves or when wearing a sword or armor, the arms are more relaxed when bent anyway. Actually, women used to rest their arms on their farthingales and panniers. This is another reason for the cast rehearsing in garments of the type to be worn during the performance. The actor will then move naturally and by the time of the performance will do it from habit.

CHAPTER 2

Our Earliest Clothing in America

1580 to 1630

Early American Costume

1580s, 1590s

A Frenchman, Jacques Le Moyne, on an expedition to Florida in 1564 painted what is believed to be the first eyewitness account of an American Indian. His painting is much the same as the one done later, about 1587, by John White of the lost colony of Roanoke.

This Indian, based on those accounts, wears paint, much jewelry, and a breechcloth for ceremonial occasions.

His body painting is red, sometimes black, and the jewelry is made of copper disks.

The disks hanging from the belt are copper but in another sketch they look like small animal tails and in another like feathers. Either the eyewitnesses saw all these types of decoration or just interpreted them differently.

Some warriors carried spears as well as bows and arrows. This one wears a gauntlet to protect his wrist. The conical hat has a row of feathers around the band with an animal tail attached at the crown. Some hats in the sketches have two tails or one tail and one large feather.

The women were clad much like those of Figure 159, which includes the Indians of Florida.

Figure 1

Englishmen settled Roanoke, Virginia, the first time in 1585 and Europeans made numerous expeditions to the east coast of America during this time.

This English explorer wears slashed and stuffed trunk hose (breeches) made up in strips and attached to a band around the leg and one at the waist. They are worn over an undergarment which is sometimes pulled out through the slashes. His silk stockings are gartered above the knees with ribbons.

His red doublet is trimmed with gold as are the hose. The sleeve seams are decorated with gold trim in front and back as sleeves had two seams at this time. Sleeves were tied onto the doublet under the shoulder wings.

A short circular cape was often worn over the left shoulder and fastened under the right arm when a cloak was needed.

This man wears a starched ruff around his neck and small ruffs at each wrist in spite of the fact that Queen Elizabeth had sent out an order to discourage the wearing of large ruffs. It seems that sumptuary laws restricting the clothing that people might wear didn't work in the Old World any more than they did later in this New World.

His sheer collar under the ruff illustrates how collars were made. It is just a straight piece which is tucked to make it curve.

His hair is combed straight back and worn curly. He wears one earring. His hat is like that in Figure 4 and his shoes are soft in the medieval style.

His sword is hung from a belt called a girdle.

Figure 2

The breastplate with arm protectors was worn by Englishmen and Frenchmen in the American colonies up to the Revolution. Here it is worn over the doublet of Figure 2 with a lace collar instead of a ruff.

The world was in a period of change as America was in the process of being settled. The invention of gun powder made armor obsolete and a whole new concept of the military resulted.

Times were changing in other ways, too, as the upper classes constantly complained about peasants wearing ruffs and bands and linen shirts like themselves.

Figure 3

Figure 4

English and Dutch sea captains wore the sleeveless leather jerkin associated with the military. This captain wears one of buff with maroon braid trim. It continues high up the neck and has shoulder wings at the armseye. Often only the top and bottom hooks were fastened so that air can get inside for body comfort. The peplum is made of several separate, overlapping panels.

The padded sleeves belong to the undergarment or shirt. They are fitted at the wrists and lower arm and then expand just below the elbow.

The new, full pleated breeches, called hose, taper to the knees where they end with decorative loops so that the fullest part is around the hips. They were padded in order to make them hold their shape.

Armor was often worn over this jerkin, either just the breastplate (as in Figure 43) or the breastplate and arm protectors of Figure 3 or with hip and thigh protectors as in Figure 30, depending on the taste or needs of the wearer.

A small crisp ruff sits on the high neck and comes up around the chin. Wrist ruffs are worn also.

His stockings are white and his tall, rounded hat and shoes are maroon. He wears a sword.

Early American Costume

English noblemen's doublets were padded and curved in beneath the stomach or belly, thus the name "peascod-bellied" doublet. They fitted snugly like a woman's corset and even had boning. The sleeves were so full and padded that a man wearing it had to hold his arms out from his body as shown. The armholes had wings.

The black velvet doublet has many small slashes or cuts in the cloth and each sleeve has one long slash from shoulder to cuff with buttons down one side and loops down the other. The undergarment or shirt shows through the slashes.

The black breeches or hose are stuffed like the sleeves, with "wool, flaxe, and cattelle's tails." They are more tapered than earlier ones and forecast the knee breeches to come.

His black knit stockings are ungartered and pulled up over the hose or breeches as they were again in the 18th century. This man wears pointed shoes of white leather with spurs.

The stiff ruff is extravagantly large but his cuffs are plain. His black top hat tapers toward the crown. This type of hat as well as the stockings and hose will return to fashion in later years. These hats of beaver were usually decorated with plumes.

This attire was often worn with the armor of Figures 3, 30, or 43.

Countrymen wore clothes on the same lines but without the elaborate slashing. Theirs were more likely to be quilted diagonally to form a diamond-shaped pattern. Quilting originally was done on doublets for wear under armor to protect the body from the metal.

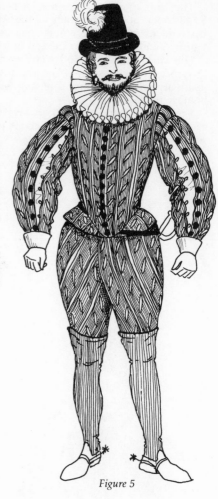

Figure 5

Figure 6

Traveling musicians, bricklayers, ordinary townsmen, and countrymen of England wore the long, loose trousers which noblemen still considered crude. Each leg was seamed down the center back. It was well into the 19th century before gentlemen accepted them. (We shall see demonstrated over and over again that the fashions of the rich are often inspired by the folk clothing of earlier periods.)

This man's doublet or jacket, like the long trousers, will change little during the coming centuries. He wears the neck open. The sleeves, which sometimes were a different color, are seamed in front and back and the split cuff is turned back. Sometimes of leather, sometimes of quilted cloth, these doublets were russet, green, or blue. Green was a favorite color at this time. His flat hat with the brim turned up is also a bright color.

His short boots lace at the side. He wears a pouch on a narrow leather strap around his waist.

1580-1600

A country lass of the 1590s dressed in a much more stylish outfit than she would have a generation before—times were changing. She might have worn "borrowed hair" (a wig) and used starch on her ruff, and even owned a looking glass and gloves!

Her fitted bodice comes to a point in front and has shoulder wings under which the sleeves are attached. Cuff-like panels are on each side of the center front of braid or tucks. The bodice has a roll or cord where it meets the skirt.

Her huge ruff which she wears high on her neck is higher in the back than in front. Her cuffs are starched too.

She wears a small roll or farthingale around her hips over several petticoats. When working she pulls the skirt up to protect it.

She wears a tall broad-brimmed hat over her starched cap which is folded back. A drawstring pouch or purse decorated with tassels is suspended from a cord around her waist. Her stockings are black and her shoes have cork heels. In cold weather she would carry a muff.

Figure 7

The English were making attempts to colonize America in the 1580s. Although the colony at Roanoke was unsuccessful, there were other visits and other attempts to form an English colony.

In time English women's ruffs grew smaller and were separate from the chemise or undergarment. The girl of Figure 11 wears her chemise open and without a ruff. The tiny-sleeved, low-necked bodice is trimmed with braid and fastened with hooks down the front. The long sleeves are part of the chemise underneath. She wears dainty ruffs at the wrists.

The open-front skirt is flared in an "A line" with a few gathers at the waist and trimmed with several rows of braid. The petticoat which shows in front is braid-trimmed also. The top one of several petticoats was meant to be seen and was always more a part of the dress than an undergarment.

This young woman wears a mirror suspended from her waist. The richer the woman, the more expensive the cord or chain. Some were of gold, or silk twisted with gold.

Her hat is similar to a man's top hat but is soft and rounded at the crown.

Expensive hats were made of North American beaver. The demand for beaver hats in Europe encouraged more and more trappers and trading companies to come to America and in a way helped to speed up the colonization. Beaver fur has a kind of sparkle to it—quite elegant.

Hat bands were beaded and jeweled and served as status symbols.

This dress can be worn with the robe of Figure 23 for a winter garment. It was worn either loose or belted with a tasselled cord.

One large painting of the period depicting people at an English country fair shows one dress of gold with pale yellow braid trim over a light yellow petticoat with black braid. Another woman wears a rose-colored dress over a blue petticoat, and still another a russet dress over a dull green petticoat. Black braid trimmed a pink petticoat worn under a black dress with pink braid.

Figure 8

19

Early American Costume

The Pilgrims lived in Holland for about twelve years before coming to the area we know as Massachusetts.

A Dutch country woman of the period wore a jacket which is a plain open-necked variation of the fashionable ones of Figures 23 and 24; these were seen in Holland a few years before the English adopted them. English women's fashions were inspired by those of the prosperous Dutch wives as were the fashions of most of Europe at this time.

This woman's apron is traditional Dutch, a square or rectangle with the ties sewn on several inches from the corners, creating an interesting drape.

Her large kerchief is tied or fastened for a few inches up the back of the head toward the crown to make a fold on top similar to some nuns' head coverings.

She wears wooden shoes, and we know that wooden shoes were worn by the Dutch settlers who came to New Netherland, later renamed New York State.

Sometimes the apron or the apron and skirt were tucked in the waist to keep them clean or out of the way while working.

Figure 9

The French settled Nova Scotia by 1605 and Quebec by 1608. Here a French vendor or rural woman wears the bodice of Figures 8 and 11 with lacings in the front rather than hooks. Like the girl of Figure 11, she wears the chemise open but with a kerchief pinned around her shoulders. Her sleeves have ruffs at the wrists.

Her skirt is trimmed with the braid bands which were so popular with rural women that they were eventually referred to as "rural bands." Reds and greens were popular colors with country folk.

Her leather shoes have pointed toes. Her soft felt hat is worn over a kerchief or fitted cap. The cap, kerchief, apron, and chemise are white.

French and German women attached the strings at the corners of a narrow rectangular apron. The front folded over and the ties in back were slightly lower than the front so that the apron stayed flat in front.

Figure 10

20

English working girls such as milk maids, vendors, and rural and servant girls wore a simple form of the dress of Figure 8 with the chemise often open at the neck. They are pictured at times wearing the neck closed and even a small ruff.

This girl wears a blue-green bodice with a hook and eye closing down the front with a red skirt and brown apron. Red skirts remained favorites with rural women for many, many years.

English women were beginning to gather their aprons slightly at the waist and increased the fullness during the coming years.

She wears a cap with a circular crown and a seam down the back of the head to make room for a bun of hair; this gives it a flattering line. The front points of the cap curve toward the face.

Her shoes are leather with high tops and pointed toes.

Figure 11

Figure 12

Children dressed much like their parents. The little girl (left) wears a red corseted bodice over a red full skirt and white lace-edged apron. The full sleeves have lace cuffs turned back over them. The lace cuffs are part of the chemise which falls out into a lace ruffle at the neckline.

Her brown shoes have red bows. She wears a flat white cap which sits on top of her head over her hair which is pulled back into a bun. She wears a locket on a chain around her neck.

This boy (right) is "unbreeched" or not yet in breeches because he still wears diapers. Children wore diapers much longer than in the 20th century. In the days before rubber and plastic pants a child still in diapers had, out of necessity, to wear skirts until he was completely trained.

He wears a padded doublet with shoulder wings and a double row of peplum panels. His shirt or chemise has a lace-edged collar and cuffs turned back over the sleeves.

He holds a hat, probably beaver (as described in Figure 8), decorated with a plume and beaded band. His little sword is attached to a belt or girdle around his waist.

21

Early American Costume

1600s, 1610s

James I came to the throne of England in 1603. He was not as restrictive as Queen Elizabeth was with her sumptuary laws which never could be enforced anyway. The English settled Popham, Maine, in 1607 but the colony failed. They settled Jamestown, Virginia, in the same year. The Pilgrims left England for Holland in 1608.

This Englishman wears a doublet with the padded peascod-belly. It has shoulder wings and twelve flaps around the waist for a double peplum or skirt. The separate collar and cuffs are made of straight strips of lace with a series of darts to give them the proper curve.

His breeches or hose are padded as described in Figure 5. They are made of strips of lace over an undergarment lining. The horizontal leg band which was formerly narrow and up under the hose or breeches is now several bands down the thigh making an early form of knee breeches called cannions.

His stockings are pulled up over his cannions. His shoes are decorated with ribbon roses.

White was very fashionable and this entire outfit is in white velvet, silk, and lace, even the shoes except for the heels which are red. It was fashionable too, sometimes, to wear gloves of another color for contrast.

His hair is worn shoulder-length and combed straight back.

Figure 13

The French settled Nova Scotia and Quebec. This French gentleman's doublet has lost most of its padding and the point in front at the waistline is straightened. This skirt or peplum is quite short but in later years is worn longer. The sleeves are capped with wings and an outer, hanging sleeve falls at the back of the arm. The seams of the doublet and sleeves are trimmed with narrow braid. He wears a small neck ruff and crisp ruffs at his wrists.

His slashed hose or breeches are stuffed as in previous years' fashions but the padding is lower and not as rounded, giving the appearance of a skirt. The lower part or cannion breeches come to just above the knee.

(A popular skit of the old Italian comedy theatre was to have a character catch his padded hose on a nail or something sharp and the contents pour out—such things as grain, rags, or cows' tails—in burlesque fashion.)

His stockings are gartered with ribbons at the knees.

Shoes have heels and tongues now. The back part of the shoe comes around and over the instep holding the tongue or flap securely in place with ribbons tied in rosettes.

His hat is a wide-brimmed felt or beaver with cord band and feather decorations. He wears his hair combed straight back and fluffed up in a pompadour.

Figure 14

The shirt survived with few changes through the 18th century. Linen was becoming more and more important and more beautiful. Clean linen shirts were the mark of a fashionable man, so much so that dashing young Dutchmen and Englishmen actually went without their doublets at times! Only a man who had on a clean shirt would be so daring.

This young man wears a soft, fine linen shirt which is so full it blouses out over his breeches top. The drop-shoulders have the sleeves sewn in with many small, even gathers which are repeated at the cuff. The lace collar and cuffs would be turned out over the doublet if he were wearing one. He not only wears a clean shirt but he even leaves the tasseled ties untied and the shirt open to show that he is clean. A locket on a chain fills in the open space.

His breeches are pleated at the waist with the pleats sewn down a few inches before they flare out and then are pleated in again at the knees where they are decorated with loops.

He wears stockings and flared-top boots with clover-shaped pieces on the instep. The boot tops are turned down showing the boot straps. Spurs were often worn with these boots.

He wears his hair combed back and softly curled. He wears one loop earring. His beard and mustache are quite pointed.

Figure 15

Figure 16

(Used until 1670s) The fishermen and trappers of the New France settlement, Nova Scotia, of 1605 started fish and fur trading companies. The trade was supposed to be with France but the settlers preferred English goods and traded with the English instead.

This Frenchman wears an interesting combination of European and North American Indian clothes. The bottom edge of the jacket is left natural and uneven but the sleeves are sewn in. The collar is part of the doublet underneath because it and the loose breeches are both red. A strip of leather around his waist holds a pouch. His old-style, short, scalloped-top boots are of green leather. Over these he wears brown pantofles or overshoes to protect the boots from the wet.

He wears fur mittens. His hat is surprisingly similar to the one worn by the Florida Indian in Figure 1. The fur brim can be turned down over the ears and the animal tail is attached at the center of the crown. A fur-brimmed hat was worn in France at this time indicating that this Nova Scotian one was probably a combination of French and Indian styles.

Early American Costume

Figure 17

(Bandoliers used until 1665.) England as well as Holland had an army of pikemen and musketeers by the beginning of the century. Muskets were used when the Powhatan Indians attacked Jamestown in 1622. The Powhatan are shown in Figures 34, 35 and 36.

The musketeer shown here wears a tight-fitting doublet either quilted or, most likely, leather. It has shoulder wings and the full sleeves become more fitted below the elbow so that they require wrist buttons. He wears the collar open with another, larger, white collar over it.

His breeches are pleated at the waist and gathered at the knee. Garters tied in large bows hold his stockings in place. His shoes have large tongues held in place by ties over the instep. A braided band and plumes decorate his wide-brimmed hat.

Hung over the left shoulder is a tan bandolier from which hang eight to sixteen black, leather-covered, flask-shaped containers of gunpowder. Each container has enough powder for one shot in order to speed up reloading. Lead shot is carried in a pouch hanging from the end of the bandolier. (He usually also wears a sword on his left, not shown here.)

The musket was so heavy that each musketeer had to carry a pole to rest his gun on while shooting. His pole, almost as long as the musketeer was tall, was stuck into the ground. The gun then had to be loaded, propped on the rest, then aimed and shot once.

One old print shows Peter Stuyvesant arriving in New Amsterdam in 1644 with a whole company of musketeers like these marching behind him. Some wear armor corselets and helmets like those of Figure 43.

The Dutch have a long history as seafarers because of their closeness to and understanding of the sea. Wide-legged breeches or "slops" have long been associated with the Dutch also. Sailor slops were the first clothing ever sold ready-made. They have been sold in "slop shops" in seaport towns since ancient times. An English sailor of 1613 was described as wearing red and white striped slops and a red stocking cap.

This Dutch sailor's blouse or shirt has wide braid trim around the neck opening, side splits, and chest pockets, the beginnings of the sailor middy. It has shoulder wings and he wears neck and wrist ruffs. The wide "slops" are trimmed with the same braid as the middy giving the outfit an Oriental character.

His fez-shaped hat has a ribbon bow and his shoes are the soft, pointed-toe shoes of former years. He probably has a dagger under his middy.

Figure 18

24

(Worn until 1620s.) When a Dutch trading ship brought women to be the wives of Virginia planters at Jamestown in 1619 some of them might well have been wearing this very feminine dress or bringing it as a part of their trousseaux.

A young English woman wears a corseted, pointed bodice, with long hanging sleeves reaching to the floor. The neckline has a crisp collar pleated like a ruff. The inner sleeves of these dresses sometimes belong to the dress and at other times to the chemise undergarment. The bodice front is trimmed with braid.

The skirt is worn over a farthingale, a doughnut-shaped, padded roll around the hips. A short skirt which is pulled under to form puffs is worn over the long skirt.

Her cap has a stiffened oval-shaped piece attached to the top which can be worn either hanging down in back or pulled up and over the cap toward the forehead as shown. Figure 23 shows a similar oval-shaped veil without a cap and larger than this one, hanging down in back.

Some drawings of this period show similar dresses with the hat of Figure 24 worn for a riding outfit.

Figure 19

English women were wearing this dress when the Pilgrims sailed for Holland so some of them probably wore some version of it. Many old paintings show that Dutch women wore similar garments (see Figure 21).

Many 19th century painters incorrectly depicted the Pilgrims in the extreme Puritan styles of the 1630s.

This English woman wears the corseted, pointed bodice and large, starched fan collar made popular by Queen Elizabeth at the end of the 16th century. Her padded sleeves are embroidered down the front and back seams. Crisp lace cuffs decorate the wrists.

The wide neck is trimmed all the way around with pointed lace (called "points") and then has a large stiffly starched collar around the sides and back. Notice the darts in the collar indicating that it started out as a straight piece of lace and was darted to form the proper curve.

Since rain or humidity would make these collars collapse, the ladies wore a collar-like wire frame underneath to hold it up. It seems that having one's collar go limp was a very humiliating experience!

This woman wears a petticoat, then the embroidered skirt, which is open down the front, and on top the short pleated peplum-type skirt. All this is over the farthingale described in Figure 19. This one is even larger. In 1613 an order was issued against the farthingale in England. Afterwards in defiance, women in England and Scotland actually wore larger ones!

While the French excelled at making beautiful intricate lace, it was the English women who were doing lovely embroidery. The embroideries of this period eventually became the American crewel embroidery.

Her hair is teased and frizzed and pulled back in a square-shaped pompadour. She wears the fashionable pearls around her neck.

Figure 20

25

Early American Costume

The Dutch first settled New Netherland in 1623. The first colonists were well-to-do merchants and traders and their wives were very fashion-minded. The Dutch trading ships brought them the very latest fashions from Holland, England, and France, and things from the Orient. The Dutch never imposed sumptuary laws on their settlers; perhaps that is one of the factors which helped New York become the center of the clothing industry in America.

This Dutch woman wears the new boned corset, much more comfortable than the iron ones of the 16th century! Only the center front contains wood or metal, the rest is flexible boning. Her bodice is trimmed on the seams with braid or wide ribbon bands. The stuffed and padded sleeves are large at the upper arm and taper to a fitted wrist. They are tied to the bodice with ties up under the shoulder wings. The cuffs are very pointed lace. (Dutch sleeves were generally larger than the French and English.)

Her skirt is divided down the front and trimmed with the same ribbon braid. Her petticoat is trimmed with a different braid. They are worn over a large farthingale described in Figure 19.

Starch was invented in the Netherlands and starched collars and cuffs became fashionable all over Europe. The Dutch tinted the starch delicate pastel tints, especially yellow and blue. Every village had its starch expert to whom you took your collars and ruffs.

This woman wears a starched cap with a high crown like that of Figure 11, but broader in front so that it stands out from the face like a bonnet. When starched, it was pulled down in the center in a point so that it formed a heart shape around the face. Some of these caps were lace-edged or made entirely of lace.

She carries a stick fan of feathers with a little mirror on it. Trading ships were bringing back folding fans from the Orient but, for a time, Dutch women preferred the stick fans.

She wears a tassel-decorated drawstring pouch hanging from a cord from her waist and a locket on a ribbon around her neck.

Figure 21

The French settled Quebec in 1608. French women dressed in much the same fashion as Dutch and English women. The farthingale was worn in France but the divided skirt would not be as commonly worn as in England for another decade.

This French woman wears a high-necked bodice completely decorated with braid. It has shoulder wings which conceal the lacings securing the sleeves. The sleeves are full at the upper arm but somewhat fitted below the elbow. They are completely covered with horizontal braid.

Her large fan collar has the beautiful starched points. The originally straight piece has been formed into a curved collar by a series of darts. She wears small ruffs at her wrists.

She wears a very long strand of pearls wound around her neck, knotted, and hanging down in front almost to the point of the bodice. Her jewels include drop earrings and a large jeweled brooch in her teased and frizzed pompadour.

Her skirt is worn over a farthingale. Several rows of braid decorate the hem.

Figure 22

26

1600-1620

Both English and Dutch women liked the comfortable flowing robes of this period, and since the English Pilgrims lived in Holland from 1608 till 1620 when they sailed to Massachusetts (by way of England), some of the ladies most assuredly were wearing them on the *Mayflower*.

This English lady's doublet was made almost like those of men which caused a great deal of criticism from men. In Figure 23 it is worn over a full skirt with the same braid trim. Her full, flared robe has shoulder wings and long medieval-style hanging sleeves trimmed with braid and lined with a contrasting color.

Her large ruff is starched and wired to stand up in back. It might have been tinted yellow or blue even though the church constantly criticized English women for using starch, especially tinted starch.

Her hair is teased and frizzed into a kind of pompadour over which she wears a veil. These lace-edged veils were just an oval of cloth pinned to the hair. They varied in size from very small to long and flowing.

Figure 23

(Worn until 1630s.) The farthingale gets smaller and will soon be out of fashion.

An English woman who might have been on the ship which brought the wives to Virginia wears the fashionable doublet and full skirt, a less corseted, more comfortable dress. The doublet is muslin embroidered all over with colorful designs which grow freer and more like the American crewel work of later date. It is decorated on the edges with gold lace.

The robe has short, wide sleeves with shoulder wings decorated with braid. The front and sleeves are also edged with braid. Many of these robes were sleeveless except for the shoulder wings. One painting shows a similar robe with a scalloped edge. These robes were not straight but flared from the shoulder down so that they flowed over the skirt easily.

She wears heart-shaped drop earrings and a narrow-brimmed, high-crowned hat with a plume and beaded hat band.

Her ruff, several layers of lace, is softer than in previous years and "falling down." Eventually these new collars were called "falling bands." Her cuffs are lace.

A portrait of Pocahontas dated 1616 (now in the National Portrait Gallery, Washington, D.C.) shows her in an outfit of this style with a starched and wired wing collar instead of the new soft ruff. She holds a stick, plume fan.

Figure 24

Early American Costume

A young English boy wears a doublet and full breeches completely covered with embroidery. The colors are blue, green, rusty red, and yellow. Embroidery was very formal at first (see Figures 20 and 24) but was now becoming freer and less inhibited, losing its confining borders. It remained formally balanced until American women made the stems wind and curl and wander in abandon over their work—until they Americanized it.

This boy's doublet has braid trim down the button front, around the skirt tabs, and on the sleeve seams. It has shoulder wings and a large stand-up but fashionably ''falling'' collar and lace cuffs.

His knee breeches are full and appear to be stuffed as were those of adults at the beginning of the decade.

His stockings are gartered with ribbon roses to match those on his shoes.

His hair is combed straight back and fluffed up slightly, the same style as men's.

Figure 25

Figure 26

A little girl wears a braid-covered bodice similar to that of the women in Figure 22 with the same point at the waistline and full tapering sleeves with shoulder wings. Her plain collar is ''falling.'' She wears crisp ruffs at the wrists, but her skirt is plain except for a simple row of braid around the hem.

Her sheer white apron has lace on the bib and hem. The bib is pinned in front, a ''pin-a-fore'' apron. Her close-fitting cap is embroidered and she wears a strand of pearls around her neck.

The little boy's outfit is almost identical to that worn by the man in Figure 14. His little doublet is covered horizontally with braid on the body and on the winged hanging sleeves. The inner sleeves are plain. His collar is braid-trimmed. His breeches or hose and cannions (described in Figure 13) are slashed, with the undergarment showing through.

His white stockings are gartered with ribbon roses to match those on his shoes.

Children's styles followed those of adults even to the hair styles. His is brushed back and up like that of fashionable men and he even carries a little sword.

28

1620-1630

1620s

Figure 27

The Pilgrims arrived in Massachusetts in 1620 and the Dutch in New Netherland in 1623.

This robe was worn by both English and Dutch men of this period. It was particularly liked by older men, scholars, the clergy, and town officials of various sorts. In fact, older men and clergy continued to wear this style for many years. It has wings at the shoulders and long hanging sleeves. These are cut straight but some of them had the same pointed sleeves as the woman's robe of Figure 23. Men sometimes wore a similar robe belted with a cord.

This gentleman wears the robe over a doublet and breeches similar to those of Figure 28 but much plainer. Instead of the crisp pleated ruff of former years his is several layers of a softer lace, with cuffs of lace.

The pointed beard and mustache are quite fashionable as is the walking stick. His shoes have straps which tie across the tongue. He wears his wide-brimmed, tall black hat cocked to one side.

Many artists have shown early Massachusetts settlers in buckled shoes and extreme Puritan clothes of a later period than the 1620s. In fact, the trading company which financed early voyages of the 20s allotted each person a wardrobe that was fashionable and even extravagant. Included were such things as lace bands and handkerchiefs, four pairs of shoes, green coats bound in red, five red knit caps, leather doublets and breeches, several pairs of stockings, garters, four shirts, two suits of doublet and hose of leather, hose and doublet with hooks and eyes, wool suits, and other things.

The two suits of doublet and hose may have been referring to the hose of Figures 13 and 14, meaning the Florentine hose or bloomer-type breeches.

Both the Dutch and the English were settling New England in the 1620s and men from the two countries dressed in this fashion.

For some years men's breeches or "hose" had been made of strips of cloth or leather which allowed the undergarment to show. Breeches have become longer and straighter and have no slashes. They have a front button opening and loop decorations around the knees. They are tied to the doublet to hold them up.

As the undergarment of the breeches disappeared, the chemise or shirt was allowed to show more and more through slashes or openings in the doublet body and sleeves. In fact, the sleeves are much like the hose breeches of a few years earlier.

This man's doublet has a sharp point in front and a high waist. The tabs of its skirt are separate, four in front and four in back. The waistline has a row of the same loops used for the shoulder wings and at the knees of the breeches. Over the chest on each side are three slashes or openings through which can be seen a linen shirt like that of Figure 15. Slashes on the sleeves stop at the elbow with the sleeve fitted on the lower arm.

Although the shirt has cuffs of its own, larger separate cuffs, split or open in back such as these, were worn too. This man wears a small ruff at the neck.

His stockings show between the breeches and the low-heeled boots which droop down. Eventually cuffed boots became popular. A clover-shaped piece of leather called a spur leather decorates the boot instep.

His hair is long and curly, longer on one side than on the other. Beards and mustaches were pointed at this time.

This costume can be made in plain dull fabrics or the fanciest depending on the characterization you want. One painting shows a man wearing doublet and breeches of black satin with yellow stockings.

Figure 28

Early American Costume

Dutch military men were sent to New Netherland (now New York State) in 1632. The first company of French musketeers was founded in 1622 so they, as well as the English, probably wore leather jerkins in Quebec when the English took it over in 1628. In fact, considering the Dutch, French, and English, the military jerkin must have been commonly worn in the early American colonies. It is known to have been popular with non-military men as well.

This soldier wears a doublet and breeches much like those of Figure 28 under his sleeveless military jerkin. Such jerkins were made of leather and usually followed the current lines of fashionable doublets. Each doublet was unique because, like hunting clothes, it was made up of a number of skins and pieces. Seams were made where the pieces fit together, with buttons and tabs added at the seam line. This gave extra strength but it was done for esthetic reasons too. Sometimes the doublet buttoned all the way down the sides but some were caught under the arms with only one button. They varied in length too.

Even the military wore lace collars and although this soldier doesn't wear lace cuffs, many did during this period.

His boots are thigh-high and flared a little at the top. They are decorated with clover-shaped spur leathers at the instep. His large wide-brimmed hat is decorated with plumes. Sometimes a short circular cape draped over one shoulder and fastened under the right arm.

French soldiers usually wore light blue jerkins decorated with a large white French cross and red breeches. The English liked buff and sometimes red jerkins while Dutch soldiers preferred yellow but none of these were national uniforms yet and the colors depended upon local preference. There was so much difference in color and decoration according to individuals and localities that a good costume designer can design original jerkins and still keep them authentic.

The cuirass or armor breastplate of Figure 43 was sometimes worn over the leather jerkin. At other times, the cuirass was worn over the sleeveless military leather jerkin over a shirt without the doublet. The full sleeves of the shirt of Figure 15 were quite dashing with the jerkin and armor although they did not offer much protection to the arms.

Soldiers carried swords and muskets and when in battle wore the bandoliers of Figure 17.

Figure 29

(Worn as late as 1760.) Many armies were still composed mainly of the bodyguards of the nobility but the idea of a king's army was developing. Uniforms were paid for by the officers so it was only natural for them to use the colors of their family coat-of-arms.

Armor was still used by some companies and until just before the American Revolution it remained fashionable for officers. Possibly some officers only posed in armor for their portraits out of tradition, but eyewitness accounts report men still wearing parts of armor into battle as late as 1760.

This style breast armor has the arm protectors attached. The hip and thigh skirts and the upper arm sections are made up of a series of overlapping metal strips (like closed venetian blinds) which will swing and move and slip up behind the next strip as the body requires.

Note the small ruff and cuffs even on this armored man.

Figure 30

1620-1630

The ladies' doublet grew more fashionable in spite of male criticism. Here a young lady who might be either English or Dutch wears one of satin with its skirt in separate panels like those of gentlemen. The sleeves, similar to those of Figure 28, are slashed the full length into a dozen or more separated sections. Inside the chemise they are stuffed to hold their shape and caught and tied with satin ribbons just above the elbow. They end in double lace cuffs a few inches above the wrist. Her long skirt is satin also.

The large fan collar which a few years earlier was wired to stand up now only flips up on the edges. It is an obvious transition between the ruff which inspired the stiff fan collar and the soft collar which came along as the stiffness was lessened. Eventually it would become a soft flat collar.

Her jewels include a pendant hanging from a pearl necklace and a large brooch on her corset at the dress neckline. She wears pearls in her hair which is combed straight back and curled.

She carries a stick feather fan with a mirror on it and is wearing make-up on her face.

The clothes-conscious Dutch never imposed restrictions concerning clothing in Holland or in the colonies. Many of the early Dutch colonists were well-to-do and quite fashionable.

Figure 31

Figure 32

Both Dutch and English women were particularly fond of this flowing style. It lasted for a number of years and even when it was no longer fashionable for young women it was still worn by older women until mid-century.

This woman wears a sleeveless robe with shoulder wings. It is fastened over the breast with concealed hooks or sometimes left open all the way to show the high-waisted, full-sleeved dress underneath. It is trimmed down the sides of the front opening with vertical and horizontal braid.

The underdress was often white with the overdress black but one Dutch group painting has one underdress in pink and one in brown. The large sleeves are tied with satin ribbons.

This woman wears a soft "falling" neck ruff made of several layers of lace and small crisp ruffs at the wrists.

Her headpiece is an oval of cloth or lace stiffened with starch. It was sometimes plain, sometimes edged with lace. The veil is separate and held in place by a pin on top of the headpiece and a pin on each shoulder. Dutch women tinted their starch blue or yellow for their ruffs and headpieces.

Her gloves may be white or pastel in color.

This robe makes an excellent dressing gown too.

Figure 33

Young boys wore skirts or were "unbreeched" until out of diapers (see Figure 12). With the skirt this young Dutch boy (left) wears a doublet like the men's with skirt tabs and shoulder wings. The ties at the waistline fasten the long skirt to the doublet. The whole outfit is edged with braid.

He wears a soft ruff of three layers of lace at the neck and lace cuffs. He is playing with a club and ball for a game known as "golf" which was brought to the colonies by the Dutch settlers.

His hair is worn in a pageboy style.

The other young boy (right) wears an outfit almost identical to that of the gentleman of Figure 28. His little doublet has the same high waist and overlapping skirt tabs which are trimmed with braid. The sleeves have shoulder wings and are slashed to the elbow. He wears a lace-trimmed collar or falling band, and lace cuffs.

His stockings are gartered with ribbon roses, and his square-toe shoes are tied with ribbons to match. He wears his hair with bangs and one side longer than the other.

The baby's dress of pale yellow with full sleeves and shoulder wings is like those of adults. The braid trim is coral red, the stand-up collar lace-trimmed. The apron is edged with lace, too, on the skirt and bib. The close-fitting cap is also lace-edged.

The shoes are yellow with ties of the same coral red as the dress trim.

CHAPTER 3

The Great Migration

1630 to 1700

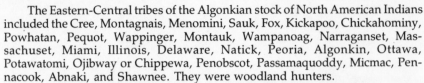

Early American Costume

1630s

The Eastern-Central tribes of the Algonkian stock of North American Indians included the Cree, Montagnais, Menomini, Sauk, Fox, Kickapoo, Chickahominy, Powhatan, Pequot, Wappinger, Montauk, Wampanoag, Narraganset, Massachuset, Miami, Illinois, Delaware, Natick, Peoria, Algonkin, Ottawa, Potawatomi, Ojibway or Chippewa, Penobscot, Passamaquoddy, Micmac, Pennacook, Abnaki, and Shawnee. They were woodland hunters.

In warm weather a breechcloth worn between the legs and folded over a belt in front and back and knee-high leggings were enough clothing. At home moccasins without the leggings were enough. Leggings were needed in the forest to protect the legs from scratches.

This Algonkin (right) wears a necklace of bear claws, a bracelet, and earrings. His hair is signed off or plucked except for a strip down the center from forehead to neck called a roach. This was cut to one or two inches in length except for a tuft at the crown which was left long by some warriors and wound so that it stood up like a fountain and waved as he fought, making him look more frightening.

In cold weather he wore just enough to keep him from freezing (left). Longer leggings which came up to the thighs were held up by one strip attached to the belt strip. They were tighter than those worn by the Iroquois tribes. The side seam was left open for a space of an inch or two and caught at regular intervals with leather strips. Algonkin leggings were always gartered below the knee.

For warmth in severe weather a cloak of two large skins held together at the shoulders was worn, sometimes decorated with small animal tails. This was worn even in snow. A heavier moccasin with the flaps turned up made a sort of boot stuffed with fur scraps or straw for insulation.

A few accounts describe some of the men with long braids. For extra warmth they wore an untrimmed whole skin of a small animal, complete with tail, wrapped around the head.

Figure 34

Powhatans attacked the Jamestown settlement in 1622 and the Pequots attacked the Massachusetts settlement in the 1630s. The Algonkian stock included the Powhatans.

This Algonkin belted tunic caught at one shoulder appears in some paintings of a later period. The fringe could be made of feathers or small animal tails.

Occasionally a tunic fastened at both shoulders, similar to that of the woman's in Figure 36, was described as being worn by the men. It was evidently the winter cloak of Figure 34 with a belt since the male tunic only fastened on one shoulder.

This warrior wears several feathers attached to the crown of his head, and his hair is shorn leaving only a roach. His bear claw necklace and metal bracelets are like those of Figure 34. His earrings are large metal loops with two, sometimes more, bead-like ornaments. His leggings are thigh-high like those shown with the winter cloak.

In the 18th century after the Indian adopted the white man's shirt he wore it belted like this with a shoulder and sleeve tucked inside, giving much the same appearance, plus a long cuffed sleeve on his right arm.

Figure 35

Woodland hunter or Algonkin Indian women wore a tunic of skins caught at both shoulders (right), belted with a strip of leather at the waist. The sides, especially the left, were held together with leather strips. Sometimes in winter the right side was stitched with strips all the way down but the left side was left open so that when sitting the thigh was exposed for use in rubbing or rolling fibers for making twines. In summer they usually wore only a skirt.

In cold weather leggings (left) were worn along with the moccasins. For warmth two separate sleeves were added, held together in front and back by leather strips. They are stitched a little at the wrists and open the rest of the way as shown.

This woman's hair is parted in the middle and braided. She wears a shell necklace.

Figure 36

(Worn through the 40s.) The 1630s were the years of the "Great Migration" of English to New England. They were marked by great extravagance in clothing. Town councillors and ministers in both England and the colonies spent a lot of time and energy protesting this extravagance with little success.

This young Englishman wears a high-waisted doublet with its skirt in eight panels or flaps. The buttons continue to the end of the flap. The sleeves have the slashes that were so preached against and shoulder wings. The linen shirt shows through the slashes. The cuffs turn back over the sleeves.

His lace-trimmed collar lies flat across the shoulders and matches the cuffs.

His full breeches are fitted at the knees and have braid trim down the side. Breeches were continually changing for a time until they finally became the knee breeches which lasted for over a hundred years.

Large ribbon roses are used for shoe ties. Ribbon garters hold up the stockings.

He holds his cape casually like a stole in the fashion of the times.

His hair is worn in bangs and long waves but wigs were tremendously popular so it might not be his natural hair.

Older men wore skull caps like Figure 55. Younger men loved the large cavalier hats of beaver decorated with plumes as in Figure 38.

In its most extravagant form, this outfit was often made of satin and silver brocade with satin shoes and satin-lined cape in pinks or white. In its simpler form, it can be plain cloth without lace and braid. The doublet was sometimes of leather.

The clothing of the Puritans was not different in *line* from the most fashionable or expensive clothing of the day. Their clothes were of the same quality as that of other people of their class—only the lace, ribbons, and plumes were left off.

Just as the fervor of their religion differed so did their attitude toward clothing. Some cut their hair short, wore no slashes in their clothes, no lace or ribbons, used only somber colors and hooks and eyes instead of buttons. Some wealthy, fun-loving Puritans looked no different from other well-to-do fashionable people such as this man. And there was every degree of person in between these two extremes. For other extreme in dress of Puritan see Figure 49.

Figure 37

Early American Costume

This Englishman's doublet is the same as Figure 37, but the skirt has only two flaps in back and one on each side in front as the coat develops.

The waist is still high and pointed in front but less pointed now than in the 1620s. Slashes in the sleeves reveal the linen shirt underneath.

His large soft collar is so wide that it covers the shoulder seam and part of the sleeve. The cuffs of the shirt turn back over the sleeves.

Fringe is used on the rather straight breeches instead of ribbon loops.

His stockings or boot hose are gartered just below the knees. The tops are wide and edged with the same beautiful lace points as his collar and cuffs. These stocking tops fall down over the garters and out over the cupped-down boot tops. (See Figures 28 and 43 for boots.) The clover-shaped piece on the boot instep is called a spur leather. The heels are high and the toes are square. Red heels were very fashionable.

A baldric ribbon is worn across the chest. Royalty, governors, and noblemen wore their jeweled crests or stars or badges of office on these baldrics.

His large beaver hat is decorated with plumes all the way around.

Red, blue, yellow, white, and black were popular colors. An outfit might include a range in hue from pastel to deep shades such as pinks to maroons or light blue to deep blue. Boots vary in shades from white and buff to black.

The clothing furnished the Piscataquay planters in 1635 included coats of scarlet as well as cassocks of cloth and canvas. Cassocks were heavy or padded coats for winter or heavy duty. The list of apparel includes new breeches to replace "the long Florentine hose of a few years before on the shores of the Bay." This does, indeed, help to further establish the fact that the hose of Figures 13 and 14 were worn in the American colonies.

In 1639 Massachusetts law forbade "immoderate breeches, knots of ribbon, lace, broad collars, capes, beaver hats, silver or gold trim, and more than one slash in doublet sleeves or bodice."

Figure 38

Dutch farmers brought their wooden shoes and loose breeches to America; they always wore their breeches looser than men of other countries.

The jerkin shown is either plain cloth in a bright color or leather. It fastens with string ties down the front. It is sleeveless but can have sleeves tied on under the shoulder wings when desired. If the farmer were poor, he would not have the wings because he couldn't afford the sleeves! One jerkin might have several pairs of sleeves. Early settlers to the American colonies have been pictured in several records as wearing both horizontally and vertically striped sleeves of red and brown or red and black.

These sleeves belong to the shirt underneath. It has the cuffs down over the hands. If the jerkin had sleeves they would be turned back over them. The neck has no collar.

The loose breeches are gartered in the same fashion as Indian leggings.

His tall black hat is typical of the period. Felt hats were worn by ordinary or poor people since the Middle Ages; the process of making wool felt is quite ancient.

New York already had settlers of so many different nationalities that over a dozen languages were spoken there. Even though the "Great Migration" mentioned in Figure 37 brought mostly English immigrants, people were coming from many other areas as well.

Figure 39

36

1630-1640

The decision to move to a new and different environment across an ocean was a dramatic and usually traumatic one. First, one must travel in his own country to the nearest seaport—which can be a major move. There he may have to spend days, weeks, and in some cases months, arranging passage. With limited funds to start with, he often finds himself hungry and desperate by the time he finally sets sail. Immigrants had to bring their own provisions—enough food to last for an entire voyage.

The clothes he acquired for the voyage when he left his home village must last not only through the trip, but for weeks or months after arriving in the new land. Even in these clothes-conscious times other needs must be met first.

But not only did he wear his own native clothes out of necessity, he wore them because they gave him a sense of security, a tie with home. When he acquired new clothes he would select or make those things that reminded him of home and of his status or trade.

This English worker—he may be a blacksmith, tanner, or cordwainer—wears a protective leather apron over a doublet and breeches much like those of Figure 17. Sometimes these aprons tie on the sides, sometimes they are left open.

His stockings are gartered just below the knees with the tops folded over into a cuff like the lace-edged ones of Figure 38. His shoes are old-fashioned ones from earlier times as is his cap.

Figure 40

In 1619 twenty Africans were brought to be sold as slaves to the Virginia planters. But it was many years before slaves were used in any great numbers.

Most servants were either indentured servants or "redemptioners" who agreed to work for a certain term in order to pay for their passage.

Prison convicts were sent from England to work out their terms also. Early colonists occasionally took Indians whom they captured in attacks and made servants of them or sold them to slave traders.

These were times of extreme interest and extravagance in clothing. Even servants and people of low means were credited in contemporary writings with having what we today would consider a lot of good clothing.

Servants and slaves who had to work in the fields were the poorest dressed because of the nature of the work. Those who worked in the big houses were dressed much like everyone else, often better than some.

This manservant of a wealthy Dutch family appears in a family group portrait. It is not known if he is a slave or a hired servant but his clothing is interesting because of its fashionable lines. It is basically the same doublet as that of Figure 37 and the same breeches as Figure 38. The doublet sleeves are shortened as well as those of the shirt.

The sleeve seams, the front skirts of the doublet, and the breeches are all edged with black braid. Black braid became in the late 18th century a symbol of coachmen's livery as the recently invented coach came into common usage.

There is no lace on the shirt and the neckband is worn open and folded back over the doublet which is also turned back. Small buttons are used on the doublet front and the front opening of the breeches.

His bare feet suggest summertime, a Southern colony, or a preference for old ways of a former life style, more a matter of tradition than economics or geography.

Servants were often included in family portraits, usually a servant in charge of caring for the children or just a favorite, trusted one.

Figure 41

Early American Costume

Many farmers and rural workers were a part of the "Great Migration" described in Figure 40.

This farm worker from the British Isles wears the full breeches preferred by rural men. His shoes are old-fashioned ones like those in Figures 2-5, but without slashes, and he wears stockings even while working.

His shirt has the drop-shoulder which will be typical of shirts even into mid-19th century. He wears the neck open and the cuffs down instead of turned back. Shirts will not open all the way down the front for another two hundred years.

His hat is the tall, wide-brimmed black one preferred by the British.

Similarly dressed peasants from France wore beautiful lace collars and cuffs in spite of criticism from the government and the wealthy—the reason, they made the lace. Who can prohibit a woman from creating lace for her own family as well as for others?

Figure 42

(Worn through the 1650s) Until James I became King of England in 1603 the principal weapon was the bow and arrow. During his reign the beginnings of a British army were formed. By the end of the 1630s the infantry consisted mostly of pikemen (see Figure 51) and musketeers (Figures 17 and 57).

This soldier might carry either the pike or the musket. If he is a musketeer he will wear the bandoliers.

He is shown here because of his long jerkin. Fashionable gentlemen did not wear longer doublets (the coat) until the 1660s. The British military influenced men's fashions around the world even into the 20th century. A man did not have to be a soldier in order to wear the leather jerkin so they were commonly worn by non-military men as well.

The jerkin, which is a doublet without sleeves, is yellow leather with dark embroidery down the front and around the skirt. The embroidery is probably red or black. The sleeves are part of his shirt. He wears gloves with gauntlet wrist protectors.

The loose breeches are rather stiff because they are made of leather also. They have matching embroidery around the legs and down the side seams.

The armor corselet called a cuirass has separate pieces for the front and back. They are fastened together with leather straps and buckles.

He wears a sword in addition to the musket or pike.

His black square-toe boots are full and very fashionable. They are dropped down to form a fold although they are not actually folded over. They are trimmed inside with lace! Notice also his spurs, the straps of which are held in place by the clover-shaped spur leathers.

His helmet is the style called a pot-helmet for the obvious reason. It has ear protectors and a chin strap. A little cylindrical socket on the front is designed to hold a plume for dress occasions.

One Dutch soldier of this period (1648) is shown wearing a yellow doublet (a favorite color of the Dutch), gray breeches, and red stockings.

The Swedes settled Delaware in 1638. The Swedish soldiers of a few years later pinned back the corners of their coattails, starting a fashion that lasted into the 19th century. The Swedes brought the idea of the log cabin to America too.

Figure 43

38

1630-1640

This young woman wears the fashionable clothing of the well-to-do. Her high-waisted satin jacket, inspired by the male doublet, has scalloped edges. Its low, square neck like that of Figure 45 is covered by two lace collars, one larger than the other. They and the soft floppy cuffs are of the lovely French pointed lace.

Her full satin skirt repeats the scallops around the hem.

She wears pearls around her neck and knotted around her waist. Large brooches were sometimes worn at the bosom.

Her hair is pulled back on top and around the crown to form a small bun. A fringe of bangs curl on the forehead and around her face. A long "love lock" hangs down on one side. All the hair is quite curly and might well be one of the sinful wigs that John Endicott of Salem forbade his congregation to wear to church in 1629. He also required women to wear veils in church so that the men would not be distracted by their sometimes painted faces during the long sermon!

Sumptuary laws were set forth in Massachusetts in 1634 against "immodest and extravagant" fashions. Some of the things forbidden were lace, gold and silver threads, more than one slash in the sleeves of dresses, embroideries, hat bands, ribbons, needlework caps, beaver hats, belts, and ruffs.

The law did rather meekly allow that this only pertained to *new* clothes. A person would be allowed to wear out the ones she or he already had.

Figure 44

The "Great Migration" of the 1630s described in Figure 40 included women as well as men who were well-to-do, of moderate means, poor, or indentured servants.

A rural woman from the British Isles shown here wears a simple version of the doublet of Figure 44. It, too, is slightly high-waisted but has laces down the front instead of buttons or hooks.

The chemise neck is worn open. The sleeves might belong either to the chemise underneath or to the doublet. These appear to be attached to the doublet.

A rural woman does not always wear her chemise open. When dressed up she will add a ruff and cuffs.

The skirt is a few inches off the ground, a necessity for country women. The "rural bands" of braid decorate the hem (see Figure 10).

She ties her apron over the doublet but some women wear it under the doublet skirts as in Figure 46.

She holds a snug fitting cap designed to fit over a topknot or bun of hair like the woman's in Figure 44.

As for her bare feet, there have been accounts of people, and especially women of the highlands of the British Isles, going barefoot as far back as the 14th century. Since many of these immigrants from the highlands chose to live in the highlands areas of America, they continued their old ways here too. America's highlanders or "hillbillies" like to go barefoot because of the hundreds of years of tradition and culture. More than one reference was made to the beauty and smoothness of the feet of these highland women.

Her hair hangs free and long, also typical of highlanders.

Figure 45

39

Early American Costume

Figure 46

A serving girl might be an indentured servant, a slave, a prisoner serving out her term, an Indian, or a woman working for an income.

As a rule, the wealthier the family, the better dressed its servants. One servant of a Dutch family is pictured wearing a brocade dress.

The doublet much like that of Figures 44 and 45 has white cuffs. The skirt is of the same fabric.

She wears her apron over her skirt and under the skirts of her doublet. It is a straight apron like those of French and German women shown in Figure 10. An interesting capelet or gathered kerchief is worn around her shoulders. It could be the forerunner of the combing jacket of Figure 79.

She wears a fitted white cap probably of linen.

The little girl's dress (left) shows a popular braid trim that will be used more and more until well into the 18th century. It has a braid down the front and around the hem. Short horizontal pieces of braid with fringed ends are sewn across the vertical braid in front. This will appear on men's coats later on.

The lace collar has long tabs in front. It is edged in lace. Her cuffs are pointed lace.

Her cap is a popular style for children that will be worn into the 19th century. It is a little turban-like cap decorated with plumes which sits on the top of the head. Her hair is curly with bangs in front.

The little boy is still unbreeched (see Figure 12); so he wears a skirt. His doublet resembles those of the men in Figures 37 and 38 except that it has hanging sleeves.

His white collar has ties with tassels on the ends.

His beaver hat has plumes on it. His hair is cut in a short pageboy style with bangs.

Both children wear shoes like those of Figures 26 and 33 with plain ties for play or ribbon roses for dress-up.

Figure 47

40

1640s

The English Civil War of the 1640s caused more people to leave home and migrate to the American colonies. But the English were not the only ones on the move. New Amsterdam already had French, Walloons, Irish, German, Portuguese, Swedish, African, and Indian citizens. By 1660 eighteen languages were spoken there!

This middle-class gentleman wears a doublet with wide slashed sleeves. It is buttoned only at the chest and left open from there down. The collar has ties with tassels or crocheted bells on the ends. These tassels will remain popular for many years. The collar and cuffs are edged with lace.

The loose breeches are gathered at the knees and trimmed with ribbon loops. The side seam is covered with braid. They have ribbon loops in front of the crotch in an imitation of the old codpiece of the 16th century.

His shirt shows through the slashes in the sleeves and in front. The shirt is shown in Figure 15. The cuffs of the shirt are turned back over the doublet sleeves.

His hair, or his wig most likely, is long and curly. It is fashionable to have a long "love lock" on one side to hang in front.

His black hat is large and wide-brimmed. His square-toe shoes have ribbon roses at the instep. The style of the shoe can be seen more clearly in Figures 17 and 27. The heel is growing higher. His stockings are gartered with ribbons at the knees.

The burgomaster of New Amsterdam, Cornelius Steenwick, is portrayed in such an outfit. Peter Stuyvesant, the director-general, wore armor like that in Figure 30 over such a doublet in his portrait. His collar and tassels were worn over the breastplate. A black skull cap like that in Figure 55 covered his bald spot. Oh, yes—he had a silver-studded wooden leg—enough to inspire any costume designer!

Figure 48

Figure 49

The two extremes of feelings about religion in England were characterized by the two groups of people labelled Dissenters and Royalists. Within both groups at any given time were people of every degree of feeling. With the Puritans, it was not a matter of being different so much as it was a matter of the degree to which they adopted the current fashions. We read of people who dressed in one manner or degree one day while associating with one group of people and quite differently the next day when with others. One diary written under Cromwell describes an official, drably dressed, whom the writer assumed to be conservative in politics. The next day to his surprise he observed the same official greeting an ambassador and wearing a red suit so ornate that "one can scarcely discern the ground color for the gold and silver lace upon it."

This Puritan wears a doublet of fashionable cut of a dull color such as black, gray, brown, or rust. Buttons at this time were made in tin, lead, wood, copper, brass, or silver on occasion. They were plain, undecorated, and small in size.

The cuffs are the only part of the undergarments displayed as there are no slashes on the sleeves or body of the doublet. The plain collar does have small tassels on the ties.

His breeches have no seam braid but they do have loops around the knees.

His boots are conservatively cupped down without lace of any kind.

Although Puritan ministers and Massachusetts laws listed capes as forbidden items (Figure 38) this Puritan gentleman wears one. These capes were made in the shape of a half-circle and worn under the collar or thrown over one shoulder or arm.

His broad-brimmed, tall hat is the one long associated with Puritans. It has no "sinful" hat band or plume and is never cocked.

Early American Costume

This man, dressed as a duke or a royal governor, or a dandy, represents the other extreme of dress in the 1640s.

The royal governor and his circle of friends were the social set of a colony and anyone of this set might dress in such fashion. This extravagant gentleman wears his doublet short in order to expose his beautiful shirt (Figure 15). Only the chest buttons are fastened. His falling band collar is lace-trimmed as are his turned-back shirt cuffs. There is an extra ruffle of lace plus satin ribbon loops at the cuffs.

His breeches are "great" or extravagantly wide. They are finished off at the knees with ribbon loops while still more loops are added on the sides. The front opening is covered with a large bunch of ribbon loops.

His boots are so flared that he must fashionably "walk wide." Getting one's spurs caught in the lace of the boot hose was a constant danger to be avoided. The tops are folded down, then up or "cupped" to hold the lace on his stockings or boot hose which are gartered at his calf, folded down and then up to conform to the boots. These boot hose were in addition to the stockings. His spurs are held in place by the clover-shaped spur leathers.

His hat is narrow-brimmed, but tall and tapered. It has both a plume and a ribbon rose plus a hat band.

His hair is long, a wig, with two "love locks" hanging in front tied with satin bows. He wears a beauty mark star on his cheek.

The Duke of York actually wore a similar outfit of purple, black, and silver with a purple baldric (see Figure 38).

Figure 50

Figure 51

(Worn until 1750s.) In 1645 Cromwell gave red coats to all his soldiers. There were red coats on both sides in England's Civil War as well as other colors, but red was becoming the favored color.

This pikeman carries a long pole used in close combat with the cavalry. The pole can keep a horse away from a soldier when it is pressed against its breast. Some pikes were as long as eighteen feet. His only weapon is a straight sword hanging from a leather strap or belt. The whole attitude of a pikeman is one of defense, to hold out, for "as long as the pikeman stands firm, the field is not yet won."

His cuirass or breastplate is straight at the waist without a point. Tassets or overlapping steel plates swinging down from the cuirass gave protection to the thighs while offering some flexibility.

The doublet and breeches are the same as those of Figure 48 but without the sleeve slashes and ribbon loops.

He wears stockings and garters tied in large bows with fringed ends. His shoes, like those of Figures 17 and 27, have ribbon roses.

His helmet has ear protectors and plumes and a neck protector in back like that of Figure 57.

The cavalry dressed much the same but with the flared boots of Figure 43.

42

1640-1650

A gentlewoman of Dutch or English origin wears the fashionable new pointed, corseted, bodice with the low neck. The front part of the corset has a wooden piece to hold the torso flat. Notice that the lacings do not cross.

The sleeves are full and have the wide cuffs of the undergarment or chemise turned back all the way to the elbow.

Her divided skirt is pulled up and back toward the rear in a drape. A white satin petticoat, which has still more petticoats under it, flows out onto the floor.

She wears two pointed collars which do not come together in front so that some of the bosom is exposed.

Her hair is pulled back in a topknot except for the sides and neck hair which is in tight corkscrew curls.

She wears make-up and a beauty mark on her cheeks.

When going out she will probably wear a hood (Figure 58) or cap (Figure 45) or both. She may also wear the cap and hat of Figure 54.

Various items are suspended from her waist on cords or chains: watches, cosmetic cases, fans, mirrors, or keys.

She wears gloves and carries a folding fan.

Figure 52

Figure 53

This woman wears the dress of a more mature person than the gay, fashionable young lady of Figure 52.

Her bodice is the same but the sleeves are long. Her collars come up high on her neck and almost come together in front—but not quite.

Her skirt is plain with no draping. Her lace-edged, gathered apron is worn over the bodice but may, at times, be worn underneath with the skirt which is tied to the corset tabs. The boned bodice is separate from the skirts. Sometimes a satin ribbon bow was worn at the bodice point like that of Figure 52.

Her hair hangs free under a long veil held by a band around her head. The veil is triangular with the middle of the base in the center front. It is pinned or fastened at the back of the head underneath. It is sometimes pinned to each shoulder or sleeve to form a drape, and probably for comfort. Women were required to wear veils in some Puritan New England churches.

Some of the original Swedish settlers of Delaware emigrated to Pennsylvania in 1643. Some of them dressed in a similar fashion.

This outfit made in black can be used for mourning.

43

Early American Costume

A Puritan woman wears a simple dress of a dull-colored cloth with plain sleeves. It is bound with a braid, down the center front hook-and-eye closing and around the waist. The braid is of the same color as the dress so it won't be conspicuous.

Her plain cuffs are the only part of the chemise allowed to show since slashes were considered sinful.

Her large black hat has no hat band because hat bands which are elaborately beaded are on the "forbidden" list mentioned in Figure 44. She is careful to have it sitting squarely on her head because a cocked hat is frivolous. She has allowed the brim to fall down in back a little.

She wears no apron although English women did. Dutch and German women were more fond of aprons.

Her collar is plain and untrimmed but the ties have crocheted bells on the ends.

Figure 54

Figure 55

1650s, 1660s

This man might be a merchant, a preacher, scholar, or an elderly gentleman.

His doublet and breeches are much like those of Figure 49 except that his breeches are gathered in at the knee slightly.

His collar and cuffs are sheer enough to reveal the darts which give them their shape.

The long gown has shoulder wings and long, pointed, hanging sleeves. It has several buttons on each shoulder seam. The gown is worn up under the collar.

This robe appears in several portraits. One of them shows it made of a sheer fabric.

A wealthy merchant would have braid or bows on the sleeve seam of the robe and braid or velvet bands down the front and around the sleeves.

He wears a skull cap. There is a portrait of New Amsterdam's Peter Stuyvesant wearing a skull cap to cover his bald spot which might be the reason for this man's cap.

His hair is long and curled. His beard and mustache are pointed. Men are known to have dyed their beards and mustaches.

His shoes have straps which come around and over the tongue. They are held with ties.

In the 1650s a wave of Jewish settlers fleeing the Portuguese in Brazil came to America. Many of them stayed in New Amsterdam, now New York; others went on to other colonies.

One small but important item became a custom—the use of the napkin to keep food stains and grease from clothing. A guest was expected to bring his own napkin with him.

44

1650-1670

During the English Civil War, English settlers continued to come to America although in the 1660s efforts were made to prevent them from leaving England.

English farmers had long worn the smock which they brought with them and continued to wear here, as shown in paintings done in the 17th, 18th, and 19th centuries. Some remained purely English in style but many took on an American character.

This farmer of New England wears a knee-length smock with a simple white collar with crocheted tie ends and plain white cuffs. The full sleeves are gathered in at the shoulder and tapered toward the wrists below the elbows.

His soft boots have a decorative band around the top and no heel.

He wears a broad-brimmed hat and a pouch held by a strap over his shoulder similar to those used by hunters to hold small game or fowl.

Figure 56

English soldiers were shipped to New Amsterdam to take it from the Dutch in 1657.

These musketeer guards were formed in 1656 by the prince who became King Charles II in 1660. He lived in exile in the Netherlands and admired the Dutch musketeers after whom he patterned his own soldiers.

This musketeer wears a jerkin of buff leather with hanging sleeves. His doublet, full breeches, stockings, and garters are all of red—the color being used more and more on both sides of the English Civil War.

His shoes are black. He wears a helmet, his only armor. It has a series of steel strips joined so that they swing down to protect the neck but have some flexibility.

He carries a musket and wears a sword held by a bandolier strap over his right shoulder. Over his left shoulder is the bandolier which holds the flasks of gunpowder, each with enough powder for one shot for faster loading. Unseen on the same bandolier is a pouch for the lead shot.

Figure 57

45

Early American Costume

Too much exposure of petticoats was frowned upon by the most devout Puritans, preachers, and magistrates. In spite of the criticism and restrictions, the draping of skirts continued for many years. The amount of petticoat revealed was a gauge of a woman's religious convictions.

The woman shown here is stylishly but simply dressed in a period when clothing as a rule was somewhat plain. Her bodice is corseted and fastened with hooks down the center front. The neckline is wide and rounded.

Her collar has become almost a cape now and is modestly fastened with bows down the front. Her chemise cuffs are folded back over her plain gathered sleeves.

Her split skirt is pulled back on each side and caught in a simple drape. The petticoat is plain.

She wears a white close-fitting cap under a fashionable hood which ties in front. The hood is made from a large half-circle with the straight side going over the head. The curved side is gathered onto a band which ties. Some had a drawstring instead of a band. The hood was usually pinned to the top of the cap so that it stayed in place. These hoods appear in both white and black in portraits and paintings.

Figure 58

A young girl wears a dress that is "old-fashioned" in some ways.

The bodice has the waist at the natural waistline like dresses of this period but with the doublet skirt or peplum of an earlier period. The sleeves are full and cuffed with the chemise cuffs. A wide collar is worn to cover the wide neckline.

Although the skirt is not divided it has braid trim down the center front and around the hem. She wears an apron which goes under the bodice along with the skirts.

The long points of her cap touch her shoulders and curve out in the Dutch style.

The dress, collar, and cuffs are all edged with braid or narrow lace or a decorative hem.

She wears scissors on a cord from her waist. Scissors were very prized possessions and were displayed proudly.

Figure 59

First worn in the 1640s, the nightgown was a new idea. It and the chemise undergarment of a fine linen are much the same.

The full nightgown is gathered at the neck and reaches the floor. The sleeves shown here beneath those of the dressing gown are much like those of dresses of the period, even to lace cuffs.

The dressing gown is full and flowing from the neck down. There is no indication of an armhole so the sleeve and body must be cut in one. The sleeves flare out over the nightgown or chemise sleeves. The collar seems to be gathered too. Both collar and sleeves are edged in lace.

The veil is like that described in Figure 53, only it is a half circle instead of a triangle.

The dressing gown is often worn at home over the skirt, petticoats, and chemise when the tight bodice is removed.

The baby wears a long dress of a dull red or brown, with a lace-trimmed collar. The sleeves of the chemise show under the little cap sleeves of the dress. They are caught twice with red ribbons, once at the elbow and once at the wrist leaving a ruffle around the hand.

The apron bib is pinned to the dress bodice as in Figure 26.

The head covering is a veil probably held in place by a little cap underneath. It is edged in lace.

Babies wear little mitts for dress-up. One account of the period tells of a red silk christening blanket with lace around the edge, beautifully mitered at the corners, and lace-trimmed mitts. Sometimes babies even wore little handmade gloves as well as mitts. One pair seen in a museum has the tips of the fingers mended with the tiniest patches. Homes and churches were often miserably cold in winter so mitts and gloves were worn indoors by babies as well as adults.

Figure 60

Figure 61

1670s

The Carolinas were settled at this time mostly by the English. The King sent courtiers to South Carolina so there were a great many wealthy fashion-minded settlers as well as many indentured servants and slaves. North Carolina was settled by English and Scotch rural people and farmers and frontiersmen from the other colonies looking for fresh lands.

This young man wears the very fashionable short loose doublet and petticoat breeches. The doublet has great wide sleeves open all the way down the front seam. They are caught at the hem with a small bow. An enormously full shirt is worn underneath similar to that of Figures 15 and 126. It has ruffles on the wristband now instead of the cuffs of Figure 15. It blouses out underneath the doublet and the shortened sleeves.

The collar is no longer crisp and is allowed to fall around toward the front. It will eventually be tied and become the soft cravat of Figure 63.

The breeches are a full divided skirt over very full linen breeches like those of Figure 57 only with more fullness. The skirt has ribbon loops over the front opening. His stockings are gartered with ribbons, his shoes tied with wide bows. His long hair is parted in the middle.

Early American Costume

Cromwell died in 1660 and Charles II became King of England; the somber period in English clothes was over. Clothes were more extravagant than ever with new styles being tried.

The doublet has been changing over a period of years and is becoming the coat that men will wear until the American Revolution with only minor changes.

This man's coat is not only longer, but fuller too, as it flares at the hem. The sleeves are short and cuffed to reveal the shirt underneath. The buttons continue all the way to the hem (see Figure 49). Only the buttons over the chest are fastened and the full shirt puffs out below. The vest or waistcoat will soon be worn to fill in the gap.

He wears a soft collar which falls toward the front. In a few years the collar will become longer and softer and more to the front until it becomes the cravat of Figure 63. It has ties with crocheted bell ends.

His breeches are full and gathered at the knee. They are decorated with a row of ribbon loops at the waist in front.

His high-heeled, square-toe shoes are tied in front over large flared tongues. The stockings have decorative clocks at the ankles. They are gartered with ribbons.

He wears a large, wide-brimmed hat that is flatter and lower at the crown. Men are experimenting with hat brims now by turning them up in various ways; in a short time the idea of turning it up in three different places will become the fashion. His hair is frizzed and curled.

He wears one fur-trimmed glove while holding the other. Gloves were given as gifts for both weddings and funerals. Fur muffs were worn in winter.

The entire outfit is of a dark color except for the shirt and collar. Red was a popular color and, of course, conservative black was worn a great deal.

Figure 62

Periwigs and greatcoats (overcoats) became immensely popular, not only with civilians but with the military as well.

Brandenburg braid trim was used with the buttons and buttonholes down the front of this man's coat. It has just one button on each sleeve holding up the large cuff. It is worn over a coat like that of Figure 65. A cravat with lace ends is looped over at the neck to fill in the space left by the wide turned-back collar.

He wears stockings and shoes with the flared tongues so high that they flop over.

His hat is turned up in both front and back and has a plume. His wig has long "love locks" in front but wigs still have a natural look. The legislature of Massachusetts denounced wigs in 1675. Ministers called them "horrid bushes of vanity" but men continued to wear them.

The Governor of New York was painted in a coat like this. He wears the breastplate armor with arm protectors like that of Figure 3 under the greatcoat with the cravat over it.

French musketeers of the 1670s dressed in almost exactly the same outfit with two bandoliers crossed over the chest as in Figure 57. One was for a sword and the other for powder flasks and pouch.

This man's hat and coat are gray with dark blue cuffs. The breeches, waistcoat (vest), stockings, and hat band are red.

Figure 63

1670-1680

(Worn through the 18th century.) Dressing gowns were worn at home over the breeches, shirt, waistcoat (vest), and cravat for relaxing or receiving guests.

This gown is made of a popular printed cotton from India. It has a plain neck with rounded corners which are turned back to form lapels. The sleeves flare and have a split at the hem which is a few inches shorter than the shirt sleeve. This can be turned back for a cuff.

Portraits by John Singleton Copley show men wearing these gowns and some of them show the shirt like that of Figure 126 with the neck closed without a cravat. One portrait shows the neck unbuttoned.

He has removed his wig and wears a cap to cover his bald head which was shaved for wearing a wig. It is a soft tam-o'-shanter with a lace flounce which is worn turned back. Fur-brimmed caps similar to that of Figure 112 were commonly worn with these dressing gowns in winter to keep the head warm. More than one diary account complains of the ink freezing in the inkwell in the bedrooms of New England homes and even of the sap becoming an icicle as it spewed out the end of the burning fireplace log!

He wears pantofles, an informal shoe with the heel open like 20th century "mules." Pantofles were sometimes made of heavier materials and worn over the shoes like overshoes to protect them as in Figure 16.

He carries a lace handkerchief and holds a long pipe for the popular pastime of smoking tobacco, called "devil's liquor" by the Puritans.

Figure 64

Figure 65

This country man wears the new coat over petticoat breeches (see Figure 61). Sometimes the coat is sleeveless but in a few years the vest or waistcoat will be worn with it. It is collarless and there is no pocket flap yet but large sleeve cuffs have developed, held in place with buttons. The pocket buttons are only decorative, never buttoned. There are splits in the side seams.

The petticoat breeches have ribbon bows on the sides but the ribbon garters are disappearing in favor of a band around the knee of the breeches as in Figure 73.

His shoes have large flared tongues. His ribbon-banded hat is worn flat in the rural fashion over his own natural hair. Rural people were not so likely to wear wigs as people in the towns.

Early American Costume

King Charles II sent his emissaries to South Carolina to form a royal colony of large estates and where there were King's officials there were always military to help enforce the laws.

During Charles's reign, red coats became established as the official color for the British armies and remained so until 1914.

Dragoons were armed, mounted troops. This English dragoon wears the newly official red coat with dark blue cuffs. It has pleats at the side seams—a developing style.

The bandolier across his chest, the belt, sword strap, and gauntlet gloves are buff. His cravat is white.

The high flaring design of the boots is to protect the legs during close formation drill on horseback. They are black and have spurs. They have a hole in the heel so that water which collects in the wide tops can drain out. One must "walk wide" in these flared tops.

His hat is a long red stocking cap with a black fur band.

Figure 66

Figure 67

Ministers complained of curling, frizzing, wiring the locks, false locks, and "heart-breakers" over the ears. One minister preached, in 1675, against the "intolerable pride in clothes and hair."

This fashionable young woman is a charming example of that "intolerable pride." Her long pointed, corseted bodice has hook-and-eye closings down the center front. Side-front seams curve down from the armholes. The flared sleeves are open at the front seam and caught at the tip with bows.

Her full-sleeved chemise shows through the open seam and beneath the elbow-length sleeves which are tied with bows.

The skirt is divided to show the petticoat in front. Both are so long they touch the floor. The gathers are caught below the seam line so that they form roll pleats of uniform size much like today's drapery pleats.

Her collar is interesting because of its straightforward construction. The lace is a straight piece which is pleated or seamed in such a way that it rounds the shoulder and falls out on the arm in a flat collar without a pucker.

Her hair is worn with a topknot high in the back (often of false hair) and long curls tied with a bow in bunches over each ear. Sometimes they are wired so that they stand away from the head and bounce when she walks. These are the "heart-breakers" and wired locks denounced in church.

50

Figure 68

A similar but less complicated dress is shown here with a series of bows, each one smaller than the one above, down the center front hook closing. The neckline is quite wide and low. The sleeves like those of Figure 67 are open at the front seam and caught with a bow at the tips. They come to just above the elbow. The chemise sleeves show through the opening and below the sleeves. A long ribbon bow hangs from the tip of the bodice.

The full, flowing skirt has the same uniform pleats at the waistline as Figure 67.

The young lady's hair has ringlet bangs and many small corkscrew curls.

She wears a skull cap with a peak in front over the forehead. This cap, in black, was worn by widows with whom it became associated in later years. The term "widow's peak" used to describe a pointed hairline came from this.

She holds a plume fan.

Figure 69

The earliest portraits of children painted in the American colonies were made during this period.

This young boy wears the short doublet and petticoat breeches of Figure 61. He even wears it fashionably unbuttoned below the chest. The full sleeves are left open at the front seam to form a slash. The full, soft shirt like that of Figure 126 shows below the three-quarter-length sleeves and below the doublet.

The petticoat breeches, like a full, divided skirt, are worn over white linen bloomer-like breeches. They have loops in front at the waist to cover the front opening.

He wears tan stockings and black tie shoes with his brown doublet and breeches.

His square collar is edged with lace. Collar, shirt, and underbreeches are all white.

He holds a walking stick and tan gloves.

His hair is combed straight back.

Little girls dressed much like their mothers but usually wore aprons over their dresses to keep them clean.

The little girl on the left wears a brown dress with full sleeves open at the front seams to expose her chemise sleeves below. They are tied with red bows.

Her lace-trimmed, sleeveless apron has a high neck and a pointed bodice with two rows of lace inserted at the low waistline. Its skirt covers the dress skirt all the way to the hem.

Her hood, like that described in Figure 58, is worn over a close-fitting cap. Her shoes are light brown with red ties.

The little dull red dress on the right has the same slashed sleeves as the other, but it has extra hanging sleeves like those of the little boy in Figure 47. Underneath the apron the skirt is draped like the one in Figure 58.

The lace collar is like that described in Figure 67. The bib of her lace-trimmed apron is pinned or buttoned to the dress bodice under the collar. Her brown and white shoes have red bows. Both girls hold fans.

Her hair is worn in a topknot with a fringe of ringlets on the sides of her face and neck.

Figure 70

Figure 71

A little boy wears a dress because he is still in diapers. Its slashed sleeves are of a striped cloth, probably red and yellow or red and brown. The skirt and bodice are brown.

His apron is sleeveless like that of Figure 70 but his has a large square collar and no lace at all.

His cap is red with a white lace cuff which curls out in the Dutch fashion.

His shoes are yellow with red bows.

The baby in the chair wears a long christening dress of dull red. Short sleeves with turned-up cuffs expose the sleeves of the chemise which are tied with red bows.

The apron is high-necked and sleeveless and has no lace. The large collar or falling band has lace on the edges. The cap has a cuff in the Dutch fashion like that of the little boy.

1680s, 1690s

People continue to seek new homes and new opportunities in the American colonies. English Quakers, German Mennonites, and French Huguenots came to Pennsylvania and the Carolinas. The middle classes triumphed in the English Civil War and William and Mary began their rule.

This gentleman wears the new coat that will remain in fashion for so many years. It is shaped to fit the body and flares out toward the hem. Pleats give extra fullness at the side seams or the seams may be open at the hem. Coats of this period almost always had braid trim of black, red, gold, or silver. They had no collar yet but the cuffs were quite large and decorative, and the top corners of the front were often turned back to form small lapels. Velvet was a popular material as well as brocade.

The waistcoat or vest had developed by this time to fill the space in front as the coat was usually worn open. This waistcoat is braid-trimmed brocade with pocket flaps.

The shirt has the new frills on both sides of the front opening (which only goes down over the chest) and ruffles on the wristband. The neckband is fitted and goes quite high up on the neck (see Figure 73). The shoulder line is low and the sleeves full as in Figures 15 and 126.

Knee breeches had developed a fitted band just below the knee where it remained for over a hundred years with few exceptions.

White stockings were becoming the accepted color for most formal wear with black for a more conservative look when the occasion called for it.

Shoes had developed a small buckle over the instep instead of the ties and ribbons. Heels were high and toes were narrow and square.

Periwigs had grown thick, artificially waved, curled, and square at the top where the hair was parted in the center.

His hat is the tricorne, the triangular shape that stayed fashionable through the American Revolution. It has braid trim and plumes but was rarely worn on the head.

Figure 72

Figure 73

Only a very daring young man would show so much shirt and breeches in those days!—a sign perhaps of the same independence and confidence that would lead Americans to demand independence as a nation.

His clothing is the same as Figure 72 without the waistcoat and shows the construction of the shirt and breeches.

For winter this coat was often edged with a narrow band of fur. One French fashion drawing of the period shows the fur from the back of the neck, around to the front, down the fronts and all the way around the hem, even going around the edges of the side splits. The coat has fur cuffs and there is fur on the hat and a fur muff!

When a man did wear his hat, it probably meant that he had a good head of hair of his own and he wanted to flaunt it, or he wanted to show that he didn't like wigs. If he did wear a fashionable wig and still wore his hat, it was probably part of a deliberate casualness, to say that he didn't care if the wig was messed up a bit—more youthful, virile independence! But carrying the hat in one's hand was more fashionable for most men.

Early American Costume

This coat is a mixture of old and new. The cravat, knee breeches, and shoes are up to date. The coat from just a few years before has huge hanging sleeves longer than the coat. His waistcoat underneath has sleeves with cuffs as they sometimes did and his shirt has ruffles at the wrist.

There is a certain conservative plainness to his hat. He could be a clergyman, Quaker, Mennonite, scholar, town councillor, or perhaps an older man. There were French immigrants at this time, too.

The man's cravat is tied with the two ends of equal length, a style eventually associated with the clergy. The entire costume is of a dark color.

Figure 74

English grenadiers were infantry who carried and used the recently invented grenades. They carried them in a pouch attached to a bandolier or shoulder strap. It was a dangerous job because the grenades had to be lit with a slow match and then thrown!

King James II convinced the English Parliament that they should support and control an army with tax money in 1688 and when they did the new army wore red coats.

The first British grenadiers looked like these, and their coats were red with black cuffs. The braid trim around the brass buttons and buttonholes is green with the ends fringed. All the leatherwork is buff except the dragoon boots which are black (see Figure 66). Some regiments were dragoons as well as grenadiers. Infantrymen wore shoes and stockings instead of boots.

The new grenadier hat was a stocking cap with a tassel and a stiff plate standing up in front. It was used in the Revolution with few changes.

The bayonet was new also—invented in Bayonnes, France, which explains the name. It was socketed in the end of the barrel of the musket. The musket couldn't be fired with the bayonet in place until in 1702 when the new side socket was put into use.

Along with grenades, muskets, swords, bayonets, and cartridge pouches, grenadiers also carried tomahawks.

French grenadiers wore dark blue coats with red cuffs, red stockings, and white braid trim. The French attacked American colonists at Schenectady and settlements in Maine and New Hampshire. In 1699 LaSalle claimed the area of the Louisiana Territory for France.

Figure 75

1680-1700

The new skirt draping became more complex as it increased in popularity.

This woman wears the latest fashion from Paris with a bodice and skirt which are all in one. The bodice has darts or tucks at the shoulder and waist in front so that it fits over the bosom. Tucks and seams are shown on the rear view. The bodice is laced over a stiff corset with a wooden front in the center. Only a single lacing is used so the laces don't cross. It is belted over the corset at the waist. The sleeves are gathered a bit at the shoulder and cuffed at the elbow with cuffs pleated so they curve. The ruffled chemise sleeves extend below.

The divided skirt is picked up at a point just below the knees, pulled around to the waist in the back, and attached to the belt. The folds are arranged carefully so that the drape is artistically balanced. The skirt has a train which creates an interesting silhouette. At times the skirt was worn straight without draping.

The petticoat with a train also is flat in front and gathered on the sides and back to accent this silhouette. Small hip pads are used at the sides.

The fontange cap is high in front and almost vertical, with lappets hanging down in back.

Figure 76

Figure 77

This lady's dress is held together in front with a concealed hook-and-eye closing instead of lacing. Some sleeves were short and flared; these are drawn up to form drapes which reflect the skirt drapes. The bodice is edged with lace and the sleeves of the chemise undergarment have bows at the elbow.

The divided skirt is pulled up on each side in a swag decorated with a ribbon rose, then the corners of the skirt are pulled toward the back and secured with another ribbon rose in the center. The lace-bordered petticoat has a small train.

Instead of a fontange this lady wears a veil edged with a lace ruffle over hair curled high in front with curls turned in toward the center on the forehead.

She wears gloves and carries a lace fan. It was very fashionable to wear ribbons tied in large bows around one or both wrists.

Early American Costume

This winter coat is one of many coat styles during this period. Some were full length, some calf-length and some long in front and short in back.

This lady wears one which is floor-length with the corners of the skirt pulled back to form swags on each side. It is trimmed with a box-pleated ruffle all the way around and elbow-length sleeves exposing the dress and chemise sleeve ruffles.

She carries a fur muff decorated with a large bow. Her cap has the stylish fontange in front and she wears beads.

Her dress underneath is decorated with wide ribbon braid. A purely decorative lace apron shows below the coat because aprons had become a part of fashionable dress. As so often happens, a folk style became high fashion for a time.

Figure 78

"Combing jackets" were short, full lacy capes worn in the mornings at home and while dressing, relaxing, or entertaining intimate friends at home. They were worn over the chemise, petticoats, and corset (or without the corset at times). Sometimes they were worn over dresses at home.

This jacket is quite full and gathered at the neck with a collar that is gathered too. It, like the apron, is trimmed with both wide and narrow lace. Some of these jackets had hoods.

The ribbon on her wrist is very fashionable. A soft veil is draped over her head.

Figure 79

1680-1700

Figure 80

(Worn into the mid-18th century) A young girl wears a simple dress for work or play. Young girls had many chores to do at home and much embroidery and needlework.

Her bodice is similar to that of Figure 76 with the sleeves rolled up. The skirt is pulled to the back to form side swags over her ankle-length petticoats.

Her pin-a-fore apron is pinned to the front of the bodice—thus its name.

She wears a plain collar over an everyday dress so there is no lace or ribbons but it can easily be decorated in the manner of ladies' dresses for a fashionable look.

Her head covering, like the hood of Figure 58, has a flared edge, much like a bonnet brim, standing up around the face.

CHAPTER 4

Clothing in the Colonies

1700 to 1770

Early American Costume

1700s, 1710s

Figure 81

Indians of the Iroquoian stock include the Wyandot or Huron, Mohawk, Onondaga, Seneca, Oneida, Caijuga, Tuscarora, Conestoga or Susquehanna, Erie, and Cherokee. They lived in areas from Canada to the Carolinas and as far west as the Mississippi River.

Iroquois leggings have the seam in front and use no fringe. This seam is usually decorated with quillwork (beads in later years). The last few inches of the seam at the foot are open so the ends fall out over the moccasin and touch the ground. One strap in front attached to the belt holds the leggings up.

A breechcloth is worn between the legs and over the belt in front and back to hang down like an apron. The front apron is usually decorated in some way.

Leggings were only for cold weather. In summer a short kilt and moccasins were worn. At home around camp the moccasins were put aside. The moccasin flaps may be worn either up or down.

The Iroquois' hair was dressed in the traditional style of his tribe. The hair was shaved, plucked, or singed off except for a strip a couple of inches wide from the top of his head to his neck.

The face of the Indian shown here is decorated with paint and he wears large earrings and a necklace of large beads with a shell pendant. He may also wear bracelets.

A strap across his chest holds the quiver for his arrows. A wider strap goes over his right shoulder to hold the pouch for his pipe and tobacco.

On cold days he may wear a large skin over his shoulders but he goes bare-chested in what the colonists would consider overcoat and glove weather.

Indian children wore nothing in summer and in cold weather only a skin wrapped around them and moccasins until they were old enough to dress like their parents.

Some Mohawk Indian men about this time adopted the white man's shirt (Figure 126.) Sometimes they wore it belted with one arm and shoulder, along with the head, through the neck opening, the long sleeve tucked inside.

For special occasions during cold weather, men wore knee-length tunics of two skins fastened at the shoulders and under the arms. The sides were fringed over the arms and shoulders forming a kind of sleeve. The bottom sometimes had deep fringe also. The tunic might be decorated on front and back with quillwork designs.

A feather-covered cap worn by men had a simple ball-and-socket pin for holding a feather, allowing the feather to spin!

Apparently, except for the Eskimos, the North American Indian did not really develop the idea of clothing made to follow the human form until after contact with the first settlers. Until then it was mostly a matter of wrapping or tying a few skins on his back to keep from freezing. He was known to have suffered a great deal from rheumatism caused from the dampness and cold.

Anthropologists will long debate about whether or not the Iroquois copied the 17th century musketeer's bandolier and pouch for his tobacco or whether he was using it before the Europeans came.

Figure 82

These Iroquois women wear knee-high leggings gartered with strips of leather (see back view). They wear moccasins with a seam in the center over the top of the foot.

This woman's wrap skirt barely meets on the left side. This allows her to use her left thigh for rolling fibers into twine or similar tasks. The skirt has quillwork designs and fringe around it.

A circular fringed cape is all that was worn above the waist in cool weather. It is slit in two places to allow the arms freedom of movement. It is often trimmed around the shoulders with quillwork designs. She wears shell beads. Quillwork was rarely done after the Indians were able to acquire beads from the traders.

In summer girls and women went bare from the waist up.

Iroquois women used a unique backpack made with a framework of willow limbs (left) which 20th-century hikers and campers have copied.

Figure 83

Figure 84

Velvet coats were popular with the neck still collarless, braid trim, and wide cuffs. Brown was a popular color.

The braid binds each buttonhole, then extends for about two inches beyond the buttonhole. It is laid under the button on the button side for the same distance so the two sides match.

Pleats were added at the side to give the coat fullness. (See Figure 92 for rear view.) Cuffs with braid trim buttoned back to the sleeves.

A sleeveless waistcoat is worn underneath; this buttons all the way to the hem.

This gentleman wears a plain shirt without wrist ruffles. His cravat is tied once with the ends hanging long over his chest. He wears stockings and black square-toe shoes with buckles over a tongue flap.

His long dark wig is pouffed out on top at each side of the part to form a square shape. He still likes to have one long lock in front.

For a duke or a colonial governor whether English, Dutch, or French, add a ribbon sash across the shoulder as in Figure 38.

Early American Costume

Pirates operated off the Carolinas, Virginia, and West Indies coasts in the early 18th century.

The famous pirate Edward Teach (Blackbeard) was sketched wearing the long loose breeches so long associated with men of the sea and sometimes farmers.

His coat is cut similar to that of Figure 84 with large cuffs but is much shorter. It has pocket flaps at the hips.

He wears a shirt with wrist ruffles. A belt around his waist helps to hold his weapons and ammunition. Two broad bandoliers cross the chest to hold his pistols. He is said to have worn at least four pistols at a time but two placed higher on the bandoliers are omitted here in order to show more of the coat.

His hat is a straw one like those worn by farmers.

His hair is braided in several tails tied with ribbons. His beard is quite long, waxed and parted into sections, each one coming to a point. It is said that he put incense or some smouldering substance in his beard so that smoke came out of it, frightening his enemies.

The Governor of South Carolina was reputed to have been in cahoots with him in some way.

Pirates were not the only ones causing trouble in the Carolinas; the Spanish and French together attacked South Carolina in 1710. In fact, the ship used by "Blackbeard" was one he stole from the French.

For the costume of sailors, see Figure 103.

Figure 85

Figure 86

The English took Newfoundland, Acadia, and the Hudson Bay Territory from the French in 1713. As a result, many English trappers returned to the wilderness in the Mississippi Valley to continue the fur trade. Many of them married Indian women. (See Figure 112)

This British grenadier wears a red coat with bright blue lapels and cuffs. All the braid trims are white. The Duke of Savoy started the custom of buttoning back the lapels (in 1664). Originally it was for comfort while parading in the hot sun, to let air inside the coat. When adopted by the British army, it was mostly a decorative feature. Eventually the waistcoat matched the lapels on many uniforms, giving color across the front and allowing ventilation too.

His knee breeches and stockings are white, his buckled shoes black. His shirt is without ruffles.

The bandolier pouch and belt are buff leather and the sword case is black.

His grenadier hat is red with a blue band around the back. The embroidery is white and gold. The early grenadier cap of Figure 75 grown taller and more elaborate has lost its stocking-cap appearance.

62

1700-1720

There was not at this time a clear-cut definition between lingerie, street wear, and formal wear—they were all much the same! Many ladies of this period in both Europe and America sat for their portraits in the full, loose deshabille or negligee. Whether or not it was dress or lingerie at this time it did in fact evolve into the loose dresses of Figures 95, 96, and 121.

In order to understand where this robe originated all one need do is to visualize the dress of Figure 76 with the belt removed, the skirts dropped down in their natural position and the bodice unhooked from the corset in front. In other words, release the dress and let it flow freely—it is virtually the same as this one.

This woman's robe is velvet, lined with satin which shows on the rolled-back flared sleeves. The chemise sleeve ruffles show beneath them. It is fitted through the shoulders and bosom, curves in at the waist, and then flares out into a large full skirt with a small train in back. It is embroidered down the front and around the neckline.

It is worn over a petticoat and corset. The chemise shows through the corset lacings which do not cross over each other because only one lacing is used.

This lady's hair is curled on top with forehead curls and a flower is added. A long curl hangs down from behind her ear. She wears drop earrings.

One similar dress in a New England museum is made of India cotton with braid trim for a less formal interpretation.

Figure 87

This robe, somewhat fuller than in Figure 87, is lapped over in front and held in place with a wide beaded belt or girdle which will reappear in the 1790s (Figure 167).

When overlapped the front is folded back to form a collar and expose the corset in front.

The sleeves are open at the front seam and rounded toward the back to expose most of the full chemise sleeve. The edges are trimmed with braid.

Underneath the corset lacings can be seen the chemise which is pulled up to form a ruffle inside the neckline.

The lady wears her hair in the same fashion as Figure 87.

One American primitive portrait shows a button on the shoulder, probably on the shoulder of the corset, to hold the loose gown in place—an idea which can be of great value in designing for theatre as well as in real life.

Figure 88

Early American Costume

This lady's dressing gown is much like a Grecian chiton. The nightgown which developed in the 1640s was more or less the same garment as the chemise.

The dressing gown is hardly more than two rectangles caught with buttons at the shoulders. It is gathered in center front and back for extra fullness. It appears to be caught in one place under each arm to form sleeves and to help keep it from slipping out of place. (If the sleeves aren't caught in this manner it will be a good idea to construct the gown this way for use on stage.) The chemise or gown shows at the neckline and sleeves.

Her hair hangs in curls with a tiny fringe of bangs. She wears no jewelry and there is no sign of a corset.

Figure 89

At this time large-scale Scotch and Irish immigrations to New England, Maryland, and Pennsylvania occurred. The English government sent 30,000 English prisoners to Virginia and Maryland, many from debtors' prisons. Many of these immigrant women may have dressed in the manner of this milkmaid, street vendor, or rural woman of Europe. Her dress is like that worn by fashionable ladies a few years earlier (Figures 76 and 77).

Striped fabrics were very popular with all classes of people. This dress is especially attractive when made of a fabric that is different on each side; then, when the sleeves are rolled up and the skirts are pinned back the result is dramatic. Also, with a vertically striped fabric the stripes will be going horizontally on the skirt swag if the fabric is the same on both sides.

She wears an ankle-length petticoat with the rural bands described in Figures 10 and 45. Her apron is trimmed with lace and worn under the skirt but over the corset tip.

Her shoes are pointed and low-heeled with flaps in front. Her bonnet ruffle is wider in front than on the sides and back.

Figure 90

64

1700-1740

Figure 91

Children's clothes often reflect styles of former years as does this little girl's dress.

Her bodice has a tucked panel in front edged with lace. Her elbow-length sleeves are flared and her chemise shows below the sleeves and around the neckline.

Even her little skirt has a train. She wears the apron up under the bodice with the skirt.

Her hair is pulled back and puffed up on top with a small fontange added. She wears a bead necklace.

1720s and 1730s

Coats of this period were sometimes still collarless but some had a small stand-up collar like the one pictured. The coat is close-fitting in the shoulders and chest and becomes full-skirted below the waist. Pockets are high but will move down in a few years. Pocket flaps have become an important part of coats. Cuffs are so large they come up to the elbow. One portrait of the period shows them even above the elbow. There is no braid around the buttons of this coat and the buttonholes are plain but braid-decorated coats were fashionable too. They were often in browns or blues in fabrics from velvet to homespuns. The fashion of the time was to button only three or four buttons in the middle of the coat.

This shirt has cuff ruffles and a plain neck opening. The cravat is tied once leaving its long ends hanging down with one of them stuffed into the coat.

His waistcoat and breeches can be matching or of a different color. His stockings are dark, his buckled shoes are black.

The wig is the familiar squared, waved style in front, but the rear view shows the latest hair fashion for men. It is a powdered wig tied in back with a black bow and the hair in a ''wig bag.''

The rear view shows the back construction of the coat with the side-back seams curving in from the armholes. These seams end in a series of pleats which make the skirt stand out, quite full. Sometimes there were splits here also.

The center back seam is split up quite high. The coattails of these back splits were almost always decorated with braid even if the front was plain. This continued to be the style into the 19th century (see Figure 185).

Figure 92

Early American Costume

Fashion not only dictates what is worn but how it should be worn. This coat is open all the way down but the waistcoat or vest has just two buttons fastened below the waist. It is natural for one to rest a hand in such a ready-made sling.

This gentleman's coat is decorated with heavy gold braid under the buttons and around the buttonholes. Each strip has a tassel at the end. Sometimes the braid is fringed at the end. This coat is olive green with gold braid. Only three buttons hold the cuff to the sleeve.

The waistcoat and breeches are the same green as the coat. His stockings which are pulled up over the knee-band of the breeches are gray, and the square-toe, buckled shoes are black.

The ruffled shirt, like that in Figure 73, is white.

His full, squared wig is powdered to a gray color. The tricorne hat is fashionably decorated with braid and plume.

James Oglethorpe who helped to settle Georgia had his portrait painted in clothes and wig like these with the armor breastplate and arm protectors of Figure 3 over his waistcoat.

Figure 93

Figure 94

One engraving of 1732 shows peasants departing for the American colonies. A written account of the period describes them as "poor, humble and neglected folk." Thirty thousand of these were prisoners sent from England. Many thousands more came from Scotland, Ireland, and Germany.

This man's clothes are the same as some of those in that 1732 engraving of a group of these "neglected folk." Their journey to the seaport town and some of their problems are described in Figure 40.

This man wears his hat flat in the rural manner. His jacket is the short, loose jacket worn by European peasants since medieval times. His knee breeches are looser and fuller than fashionable ones as is characteristic of rural clothes. His shirt is without a collar and open at the neck.

His shoes fasten with ties instead of the new buckles. His clothes are those of another generation but it is not entirely his poverty that causes this. Rural people have, through the ages, held onto styles longer than people in the cities so his clothes are a result partly of tradition and heritage, partly of his misfortune in life. This holds true also of the custom of going barefoot described in Figure 45.

This sacque dress is much like Figure 87 especially in the front but the back is the newest fashion.

The buttons are left open above the waist to show the ribbons on the corset front and then buttoned from there down. The sleeves are short and reveal the chemise sleeves underneath. The dress is rather complex because it is somewhat fitted and curved in at the side underarm seams, comes around still close fitting toward the center back, and then meets in a series of large pleats that fall from the neckline into a skirt train.

Caps at this time are snug and untrimmed, hardly more than a handkerchief drawn up with a few gathers. They, as well as hair styles, are undramatic.

In one contemporary engraving several of these robes appear in a shorter length (about to the knees) in an outdoor scene, indicating they are coats over dresses. One has an apron on the front of the skirt which extends below. All the women wearing these coats are wearing the flat bonnet of Figure 105.

Figure 95

Figure 96

A young lady is dressed in printed linen with a bodice fitted over a corset in front and a back fullness like that of Figure 95. These dresses were made on a lining which fits the figure and serves as the form on which the outer dress is pleated and draped.

The bodice has the pleat which comes from the shoulder and is stitched down alongside the corset front. The corset front is decorated with bows which, as in Figure 95, decrease in size toward the point. One large bow with long streamers finishes off the point of the bodice.

The sleeves which cover the elbow have a pleated cuff which curves to fit the arm. This cuff was worn to the end of the 18th century.

Her chemise undergarment forms ruffles at the neckline and sleeves.

Her skirt is full and up a few inches off the floor although many of these same dresses were floor-length and with trains.

Curved points on her starched lace cap indicate it might be Dutch or German.

Her shoes have pointed toes which turn up slightly, flared heels, and a buckle across the instep.

(Worn through the 1770s) For a time diagonally fastened bodices were the vogue. Frog fasteners were often used for closings. The chemise and corset lacings show at the neckline of this pastel satin dress. The sleeves are short and flared to reveal the chemise sleeves which have ruffles deeper on the underside than on top so that they hang down in back.

The plain skirt is worn over a small hoop. Hoop sizes will increase in later years.

The cap is quite small and close-fitting over hair which is pulled back in a loose bunch of curls in the back.

Although this style was worn for a short time in Europe it appears in American portraits on through the 1770s sometimes with sleeves like those of Figure 88, but a few inches shorter.

Figure 97

This rural German woman is representative of the many German immigrants who came to the colonies during the early part of the 18th century. These people settled in all the colonies but especially in the Hudson Valley, Pennsylvania, Virginia, and the Carolina back country.

Her corset is worn on the outside of her bodice jacket which has elbow-length sleeves. The chemise is high at the neck. She has rolled up her sleeves which show below the bodice sleeves.

The corset is laced with a zigzag lacing which does not cross over itself. It is edged with braid or narrow lace.

By tradition, through the years rural women's skirts have been a few inches off the ground as this one is. Her apron is a straight narrow one.

She still wears the old soft, pointed-toe shoes of former years. A close-fitting cap of white is worn under the dark cap which has starched points that turn out. It has a peak at the forehead.

Figure 98

(Worn until mid-19th century) A European country woman wears her corset or body without the sleeves which are tied in. Some rural women apparently never wore the sleeves and still others wore the body over a jacket like that of Figure 98. (What appears to be a jacket is often just the body with the tabs on the outside of the skirt. See Figure 107.)

Part of the chemise neck ruffle shows across the neckline and then is covered at the shoulder by the corset strap. The chemise sleeves are long and full. The corset is edged in a dark braid all the way around.

Rural bands decorate her shortened skirt as in Figures 10, 45, and 90. These skirts are often made of calico. The same braid used on the corset edges was used for her apron.

She wears a fashionable bonnet with a gathered frill around her face and a ribbon around it. Her buckled shoes are more fashionable than those of Figure 98.

An eyewitness sketch dated 1850 of immigrants going through the Appalachians on the way west shows several dresses identical to this one. It is certain there were many such dresses in the colonies through the 18th century and beyond mid-19th century.

Figure 99

Figure 100

A little boy wears a coat like that of men of the period. He even has it buttoned in the current fashion. It is collarless, with large cuffs and pocket flaps with the same braided buttonholes as the front.

His little shirt is like that of Figure 73 and he wears a cravat tied in still closer imitation of grown-up men.

His knee breeches, stockings, and square-toe shoes as well as his hair complete his "little man" outfit.

1740s

(Worn through 60s.) The coat became double-breasted with a large collar in the 40s. The cuffs were large, almost to the elbow. The pocket flaps were lower than a few years before.

This man's waistcoat is buttoned at the chest, left open over the stomach, then buttoned for a few buttons just below the waist. This is done for ventilation but it also happens to be fashionable. At times the ends of the long cravat were pulled out through the opening.

The waistcoat now always has pocket flaps as well as the coat.

His shoes have large tongue flaps and large metal buckles. They are black, his stockings are dark. He carries his gloves.

The double-breasted, large-collared coat became the uniform of the British naval officers in 1748 so it was worn by both civilians and military. England sent ninety vessels out of Boston to besiege Fort Louisbourg so there were, one would assume, at least ninety British naval officers or more on this expedition.

Officers' uniforms usually used braid trim along with lapel facings, cuffs, and collar of a contrasting color. They often wore the double-breasted vest of Figure 115 with much gold braid trim. The uniforms usually were red with medium blue facings and gold braid edgings.

This man's hair is natural but worn in the style of fashionable wigs.

Figure 101

Figure 102

(Worn through the 18th century) England, Holland, and Austria fought against France, Spain, and Prussia in what was called King George's War.

This robe, with minor differences, was worn by government members in both England and France and by the clergy of many religious groups. Unless the robe of a specific religious order or sect is required or some particular judicial or governmental rank is called for in your script, this robe may be used in one of its many variations.

Such robes appeared in numerous political cartoons and paintings throughout the 18th century. Sometimes the sleeves were gathered at the wrist as shown, at other times they were loose and flared. Occasionally the robe was longer in back so that it made a train about 12" in length.

One painting shows Ben Franklin, in 1774, before the Privy Council in England. Two of the officials wear black robes and white wigs as shown here. Some wear red sleeveless robes or red robes with white collars and a large blue bow on each shoulder.

One political cartoon shows this robe in white with a black sleeveless one over it. Some robes were all white with black bands around the neck similar to professors' hoods. There were black sleeveless robes, too, and in one cartoon an official, obviously representing the Highlands, wears a plaid stole over his right shoulder and a Scottish bonnet on his head (see Figure 140 for bonnet).

The Highlanders had lost their fight for independence from England and, as punishment, England sent many of them to the American colonies. (For Scottish military uniform, see Figure 140.) Jewish settlers came from England at this time, too.

This man wears the clothing of a sailor, a peasant of Europe, or a laborer. He might be newly arrived in the colonies from a debtors' prison.

His breeches are the pantaloons or slops long associated with sailors and farmers. For centuries upper classes have adopted as fashionable, styles of folk clothing that they looked down on as crude only a few years earlier. Eventually in the early 19th century the pantaloon became the fashion but at this time, the 1740s, it was still in its folk form.

His short jacket is the timeless coat with few changes shown in Figures 6, 39, and 127.

His striped stockings, buckled shoes, and kerchief are up-to-date. The way he wears his kerchief or cravat is almost identical to those in Figures 140 and 141.

His stocking cap hasn't changed much since the early Puritan's clothing allotment included "red knit caps." These stocking caps were made by simply tying a string around one end and leaving a topknot or turning the knot to the inside.

Figure 103

Figure 104

After the English with American help took Fort Louisbourg, the French tried to burn Boston as punishment but failed in the attempt. The American colonists were infuriated when the English then traded Fort Louisbourg back to the French for a port in India in 1748. Resentment against the British was beginning to build up in the colonies.

British Buffs were called this because of the buff facings and waistcoat of their uniform.

This soldier's coat is red. The lining, waistcoat, facings, and cuffs are buff with red braid trim. The coattail corners are left plain. The lapels are buttoned back and for the first time the tails of the coat are turned back.

His breeches are red and his white leggings come up midway over the thighs. They are often worn with garters as shown on his left leg.

The bandolier or shoulder strap and pouch and the belt are buff leather.

His shirt is like that of Figure 126 with small wrist ruffles.

He wears the black tricorne hat edged in white but some Buffs are pictured wearing the grenadier hat of Figure 86.

Some of the officers are shown wearing the armor of Figures 43 or 51.

Early American Costume

(Worn into 1780s) Self-ruchings, or small double ruffles, trim the neck opening and bodice front of this dress, covering the hook fastenings. The below-the-elbow-length sleeves are shaped so that they are longer at the back and curve up in front to fit the bend of the arm. They are trimmed with a self-ruffle. A predominantly green, flower-printed linen is used for the bodice and skirt.

The neck ruffle of the chemise is pulled up so that it shows just inside the neckline ruching. The chemise sleeve ruffles hang out underneath the bodice sleeve ruffles. Some sleeves of this period have several ruffles.

Small panniers at the hips are formed by drawing up the skirt in drapes. Hoops are worn underneath (see Figure 107).

Her muslin quilted petticoat has flower and leaf designs with a diamond-shaped allover background pattern. This is an early example of an art (quilting) that will increase in popularity (see Figure 118). Satin was used for quilted petticoats also.

A flat, circular straw hat sits on top of her head. It is decorated with flat cloth flowers and a little lace edge. One similar hat was made of cloth and decorated with crewel embroidery. Sometimes these flat hats were worn over a white cap. They have little more than a suggestion of a crown.

Her hair is pulled back and held close to the head and neck in a loose knot. She wears a bead necklace.

Women's coats of this period were much like the dress of Figure 95.

Figure 105

(Worn to 1780s.) The bodice of this lady's satin dress hooks down the front to the point. Elbow-length sleeves are flared with small scallops on the edge. The chemise sleeves are longer than the bodice sleeves and made so that the ruffle is longer at the back causing it to hang most prettily.

Although the skirt is not open in front as many were at this time it does appear to have a seam in front.

Her soft kerchief covers a neckline like that of Figure 105. It falls around the shoulders with a deliberate casualness, then goes under ribbons which secure it with a large bow in front. The ends of the kerchief hang down beyond the tip of the bodice point. The ribbons are fastened or pinned to the bodice so that the carefully arranged but casual-appearing folds will stay in place. (See also Figure 119.)

The head covering which looks like a veil is really a bonnet. It is gathered slightly and repeats the chemise sleeve design with more ruffle hanging in back than in front. Some caps of the period still had lappets in back like those of Figures 76 and 107, although they were not worn much by young women except at home.

A drawstring bag with braid and tassels holds personal articles such as face powder, patches, rouge pot, perfume case or mirror.

Her necklace is a short strand of pearls, not necessarily genuine since paste or imitation jewels were so popular they were worn even by the wealthiest women during the 18th century.

Figure 106

Figure 107

Ladies' dresses and undergarments were in a number of separate pieces. There was no clear-cut definition of what was clothing and what was underwear until the 19th century. At this period the undergarment was merely the part of the costume worn under the outer garment. It was not something to be hidden but just another element of the total costume.

The body was often two pieces, open down the front and down the back. The term "bodies" eventually became "bodice." Sometimes it opened just in the front with hook closings or laces, sometimes just in the back. It was made of the same fabric as the dress and boned at a number of places all the way around. The center front of the bodice had a wedge-shaped pocket (indicated by stitching lines) for inserting a busk or wedge-shaped piece of wood covered with beautifully embroidered cloth (on floor). The body, also called a stay or corset, has small tabs on the bottom from the side front around to the back which go inside the skirt to stabilize it (Figure at left). Sometimes they are fastened to the skirts. There are no tabs in front under the busk which goes on the outside of the skirt most of the time.

The stays or strips of boning (indicated by stitching lines on body, left) are put in diagonally rather than vertically, which makes them not only more comfortable but actually more effective. The ties on the armhole are for holding the sleeve to the body. Notice the curved shape of the sleeve in the woman's hand with its two seams rather than just one. Some sleeves were sewn to the body, some were tied on as all sleeves had been in former years. Some corsets, especially in Europe, were cut low under the bosom as in Figure 99.

Her hoop is gathered at the waist only on the sides. The boning, which at various times in history has been flexible steel or basket reed, is sewn into the petticoat in several rows. These vary in length from hip-length to ankle-length. A piece of boning is put in diagonally from front to back across the hip so that the hoop is held broad at the sides but flat in front and back. The whole thing swings suspended from the drawstring waist.

The woman on the right wears the chemise, petticoats, and dress skirt without the corset body. Over this she wears a soft, full cape sometimes called a combing jacket, and worn at home for relaxing without the tight corset.

Her cap is like that of the woman on the left but with lappets like those of Figure 76.

The chemise which also serves as a nightgown has a drawstring at the neck with a standing ruffle edge, sometimes lace. The drawstring is the secret to making the ruffle edge always conform so perfectly to the body neckline. It is drawn up to the correct size, then pulled and arranged meticulously until it appears to be sewn that way. The "peasant blouse" of the 20th century is a modern version of this chemise.

She is holding an embroidered pocket worn under the petticoats for holding cosmetics, snuff, head scratcher, fans, gloves, keys or whatever she might need. It, too, is tied around the waist and is reached through slits in the skirt. All these skirts, pockets, petticoats, and aprons worn around the waist create so much bulk that the busk in the body front is necessary to flatten it all down in front.

Stockings were held with garters below the knee at this time.

73

Children's clothes still imitate adults' although that will change in a few years. This young girl's bodice is like that of Figure 105 but without trim of any kind. It closes with hook fasteners down the front. Her sleeves, which end at the bend of her arm, have cuffs which are pleated to curve with the arm. No chemise ruffles show at either the neck or sleeve.

Her apron bib is pinned onto the bodice which gives it the name pinafore. The bib is shaped slightly wider at the top than at the waist. It has a long gathered skirt over a plain dress skirt.

She wears mitts and a bonnet which seems to be made of a half circle rather than a whole one. It is gathered across the front and sides of the face but goes up in back. Her hair is worn in a bunch of curls high in back like a 20th century ponytail that fits into the point of the cap. Her shoes have buckles.

Figure 108

Figure 109

(Worn throughout the 18th century) Boys' coats are like those of men, as shown in Figure 92. This boy's cuffs have just one button on the sleeves to hold them up. His shirt is like that of Figure 126.

The most interesting part of his costume is his striped apron. It is about a yard square with two corners cut off making a pointed bib. It could be a square with the two corners merely folded under. The point has a buttonhole and buttons onto one of the buttons on his coat. It is belted with a cord or leather strip wrapped around twice.

His buckled shoes and dark stockings are like those of men of the period.

His hair is pulled back in a black bow and bag like Figure 92 but his is tied high up on the back of the head more like a 20th century ponytail. The hair around his face is cut short in a fringe of curls, probably to keep it neat while playing.

The drawstring bag he holds is the school bag of the period for his books.

This apron that buttons onto the coat was also worn by men, as paintings of this era record.

1750s, 1760s

Men's clothing, which went through various changes at the turn of the century, changed little until after the Revolution.

The most obvious change in men's coats was in the cuffs of the sleeves. This gentleman wears a red coat with a green collar and a green waistcoat. Gray collars and waistcoats were popular too. Waistcoats were becoming shorter. Coat cuffs were now slits in the sleeve which buttoned with either three or four buttons.

The breeches of this gentleman are buff. The shirt is like that of Figure 73.

He wears high English boots with a turned-down cuff of buff canvas lining. This boot will be worn for riding in the 20th century and will be the jockey boot.

Two rolled curls are worn over his ears and the rest of his natural, lightly powdered hair is tied in back with a ribbon. The periwig is no longer in style.

Hats like this braid-trimmed tricorne were really worn again instead of just carried.

A similar coat of the period is dark red with a gray lining and collar, worn with a gray waistcoat and buff breeches. Some coats still have cuffs and when they do they match the color of the collar.

Figure 110

This young man, probably a student, is conservatively but tastefully dressed. The coat is not as full as those of a few years ago and is just beginning to curve back slightly—a hint of what is to come. The collar is large and soft. Only three buttons are used on the slit in the sleeve.

He wears the shortened waistcoat. His stockings are pulled up over the knee band of his breeches. Sometimes the stockings are buttoned into the breeches buttons.

The buckles of his square-toe shoes are large while the flap has become a little smaller.

His hat is the tricorne with braid trim. His hair with one roll over the ears and pulled back in a ribbon is his own natural hair.

Figure 111

Early American Costume

(Worn until mid-19th century) The farmer's smock (Figure 56) meets the Indian's tunic in the wilderness and becomes the hunting shirt of linen or buckskin. Long fringe was not practical in the forest where there were too many things for it to snag on; so early hunting clothes had very short fringe.

The 1750s brought the beginning of the French and Indian War and although the British military wore their new red coats, by which they would become so identified, the Americans who fought alongside them used their hunting clothes.

These smocks, tunics, or long shirts were individual in style, made by a wife or even by the hunter himself. Some were made by Indians. The linen fringe was often dyed blue, green, or brown. One smock in a painting of Braddock's men at Fort Duquesne is natural with blue fringe. Sometimes the entire smock was dyed blue, green, or brown; in fact, blue was a popular color for hunting smocks or shirts until the Civil War.

In the same painting, one man wears his smock belted and with a shoulder strap and pouch like that of Figure 113.

Knee breeches, stockings, and buckled shoes were often worn with the smock but both the French and English armies in the Ohio Territory preferred leggings or boots. On military expeditions, the leggings were more likely to be worn. For wilderness travel Indian leggings were best. (Color plate No. 1)

The hat is the traditional fur-brimmed soft hat which Frenchmen favored for many years both in the colonies and at home. It could be turned down over the ears in cold weather.

The French army fought in deerskin clothes alongside their allies, the Indians, so that they looked much the same. The Britishers' new red coats proved to be excellent targets for the French and Indians in the early years of the war.

Figure 112

(Worn until mid-19th century) In winter, animal skins were used for hunting clothes. Linen was used for the warm weather ones. In many engravings, cartoons, and paintings, it is difficult to tell for sure whether those pictured are linen or deerskin because they are so similar in color and texture when portrayed on artist's canvas or paper. The animal skin clothes were pieced together from small pieces of skin and a few artists showed these seams in their work. But homespun cloth was precious so linen clothes were pieced together from every usable scrap too. Linen, like skins, might have seams almost anywhere.

Fringe was sometimes used to cover a seam, especially where water might seep through. Fringed seams divert and break up the water into droplets and drain it off so the fringe was practical as well as aesthetic. Linen fringe has more of a tendency to tangle than that of the animal skins and makes a more rounded, brush-like fringe.

Men who trapped, traded, or hunted in the forests for any great length of time adopted the Indian leggings and moccasins. These offered best protection for the legs. A man could only carry so much in a small pack so when a shoe wore out or a legging was torn he repaired them himself or bought or traded for new ones from the Indians. See Figure 145 for a combination of Indian and gentlemen's clothing.

The early leggings were probably held up by a strap as in Figures 34, 81, and Color plate No. 7, and worn over the knee breeches.

Shirts and smocks did not open all the way down in the front. This man wears a white shirt with a black cravat tied in the back like Figure 141. Sometimes a black ribbon was tied around his neck and the ends of it tied around his hair.

His hat we have seen before: The early Indians of Florida (Figure 1) wore a round hat with an animal tail attached to the crown. The early French settlers of Nova Scotia wore a similar hat in 1605 (Figure 16) and the Algonkin Indians wrapped an animal skin, complete with tail, around their heads (Figure 34). Apparently hats of this type have long been worn by Indians along the entire eastern coast of North America. This is the hat that eventually became the American hunting or coonskin cap associated with the pioneers of Kentucky and Tennessee.

Figure 113

Early explorers described the forests of North America as jungles and indeed they were and are. The colonists learned about the forests from experience and from the Indians. The British learned that fighting in the virgin forests of North America was not like fighting on the battlefields of Europe so they designed a new uniform especially for this terrain. The British North American Light Infantry uniform had a shortened coat of red with dark blue cuffs and steel buttons. A combination of breeches and Indian leggings to protect the legs became something new in military uniforms: long buff trousers with foot straps.

The cap has a flap for the ears and can button under the chin in cold weather.

Another new idea in military wear was the backpack, perhaps inspired by those made and used by Iroquois women. The backpack included the bed roll and a longer coat for cold weather.

One strap across the shoulder held the cartridge pouch and a tomahawk while the other, over the left shoulder, secured a canteen and powder horn.

Figure 114

Figure 115

In 1768 a British fleet anchored in Boston harbor and four regiments of British soldiers debarked and marched through Boston.

Later when a private American ship was seized, angry crowds of Bostonians managed to get one of the small British boats to Boston Common and burn it!

A British naval officer of this time wore a dark blue coat with a collar and wide cuffs which buttoned vertically instead of across the cuff. The front corners were cut away indicating the coming trend.

His white waistcoat was double-breasted with brass buttons, edged in flat gold braid, and decorated with gold embroidery as well. It could be worn as shown or each side could be folded back and buttoned to its own side like a military coat.

He wore white breeches, white stockings, and black shoes with large buckles. His tricorne has gold braid trim.

This was not actually an official uniform. It was an outfit worn by a naval officer while uniforms were still subject to individual taste. An officer might wear the double-breasted coat of Figure 101 as an alternative.

Early American Costume

Although some regiments of the French cavalry wore blue and the King's own regiment red, most French infantry regiments were now wearing white in spite of its demoralizing effect where wounds were concerned. (It was discontinued by 1811 for this reason.)

This French infantryman wears a white coat with a small collar and rather large cuffs of black. It is single-breasted. The coattails, also white, are buttoned back. All the buttons are brass except the ones on the tails which are bright red.

His breeches, gaiters, and waistcoat are also white. The gaiters or leggings were sometimes gartered below the knee.

He wears a red grenadier hat with a black fur plate in front. The custom of braiding the hair in one large braid in back and a small braid on each side is an interesting one. The men of the Muskhogean Indian tribes had long done this as shown in Figure 158. The Muskhogeans were the southern farming Indians. The French attacked the Carolinas in 1710 when so much pirateering was going on along the same coast in Muskhogean territory.

The famous pirate "Blackbeard" wore the side pigtails or braids to add to his frightening appearance (see Figure 85). Perhaps the French and "Blackbeard" got the idea originally from these southern Indians.

His sword hangs from a shoulder strap instead of a belt and has a red tassel decoration.

The Marquis de Montcalm who led the French at the Battle for Quebec wore armor like that of Figure 43 under a velvet coat in his formal portrait.

Figure 116

Figure 117

The British North American Light Infantry uniform (Figure 114) which was designed for fighting in the forest was used in the more remote areas earlier in the French and Indian war. More traditional uniforms were sketched in eyewitness accounts of engagements at Crown Point and Ticonderoga on Lake Champlain and the Plains of Abraham above Quebec in 1759.

British grenadiers such as this one (left) appear in almost all contemporary accounts of this time. He wears a collarless red coat with yellow lapels, cuffs, and lining. It is trimmed with white braid and steel buttons. The shoulder wings are of an earlier period. The waistcoat is red with braid trim and the breeches are red.

The tall grenadier cap is yellow with white braid. Its embroidery is red and white. There is a pompon on the tip of the point.

His thigh-high leggings are white, over black shoes. Shoulder straps are slightly narrower than in former years.

A dragoon officer (right) wears a red coat with braid trim and steel buttons but it has neither collar nor lapels. The braid is in chevron or "V" shaped designs on the hips and cuffless sleeves. He has epaulettes on the shoulders; enlisted men do not have them.

The waistcoat and breeches are buff. His white stockings are pulled up over his breeches to just above the boot tops.

Since dragoons are mounted troops he wears riding boots. They come just to the bend of the leg in back, then curve up abruptly toward the front where they go above the knee. This gives knee protection but at the same time eliminates the bulk in back when the leg is bent.

He wears the tricorne hat with a cockade and braid trim.

Major General Amherst who led the English forces at the Battle for Quebec in 1759 wore the armor of Figure 30 in his formal portrait. Whether or not officers at this time actually wore armor during battle we can't be sure, but there is no doubt at all that they wished to be remembered dressed in armor.

78

A man fights with more determination when he has a home with a wife and children to fight for. And, while this helped the English colonies to win in the French and Indian War, in a few years it was part of the reason for their winning in a revolution against England.

These wives, and mothers, and daughters were doing more than just inspiring their men by being charming. They quietly began to defy the restrictive laws against home manufactures imposed upon colonists by England and would more openly defy them in the coming years.

This woman wears a linen dress with a divided skirt. The bodice is laced in front over the chemise which has a ruffle around the neckline. The sleeves are quite short and reveal fitted chemise sleeves which are longer but still above the elbow. They have a ruffle which is longer in back than in front.

The skirt, open in front, has crewel-embroidered panels down each side. It touches the floor. The shorter petticoat, quilted in a floral design, is a work of art.

Quilting was done during medieval times in Europe and China to wear as padding under armor. The women of colonial America turned this utilitarian padding into works of art now shown in the finest museums. But the ladies quilted their petticoats to make themselves warm, pretty, and fashionable, not for museums (see also Figure 105). Favorite fabrics for quilted petticoats were plain muslin and white satin.

This woman's hair is lightly powdered, frizzed, and teased into a small pompadour. Sometimes bows or flowers are added to the hair.

Figure 118

Figure 119

American women, possibly because of the Puritan influence, always loved their white caps and collars or kerchiefs.

This woman wears a bodice with a hook-and-eye closing in front. The sleeves come to just below the elbow and have cuffs which are pleated horizontally to fit the elbow. Her chemise sleeve ruffles show below the sleeve cuff.

The most interesting part of this costume is the way in which the triangular kerchief is worn. The bodice front has two ribbons attached at the bosom which tie across the kerchief. The folds of the kerchief are never accidental even though they appear so. Every fold is carefully arranged in order to achieve the proper drape. The kerchief ends hang freely.

The older or more modest the woman, as a rule, the higher she wore her kerchief. More daring younger women were apt to arrange it so that "accidentally" it revealed more.

She wears her bonnet tied under her chin with the ruffle continuing under the chin and thus encircling the face.

Color Plates

All the black and white figures were taken from historical accounts either visual or written. Some are quite literal interpretations and some are composites in cases where a great deal of material was available. They are meant to be used as a reference for your own designs. The color plates, I hope, will serve to demonstrate how you can use the drawings, together with the suggested variations and historical facts accompanying them, and adapt them to your own special needs. When you do this you will, in a sense, be doing the same thing that the historical individuals and groups did when they adapted the current fashions to their own special needs in real life.

After you adapt the factual material to a certain type of individual as I have done, then you are ready to adjust it to suit the age, personality, physical build, class, etc. , of the particular character in your script who will wear it.

Theatre in America is growing more popular and more professional every day and will continue to do so in the future. Those of us who care about good theatre and good costumes have a wonderful challenge ahead of us! We must work to make our plays more exciting, informative, and beautiful than they have ever been so that each person who comes to experience theatre will want to return.

Plate 1

Plate 2

Linen hunting shirts or smocks of the early 18th century (described in Figure 112) were sometimes worn with a belt, shoulder strap, and cartridge pouch. Deerskin Indian leggings over the knee breeches were preferred for use in the wilderness because they offered comfortable protection for the lower legs.

During the French and Indian War both the colonial and French soldiers fought in similar smocks. Frenchmen preferred the fur-brimmed hat while Americans favored the tricorne as shown. Green fringe was usually used by the colonists, a tradition which goes back many years in rural England. Frenchmen often dyed their fringe blue.

The everyday work outfit consisting of open waistcoat with no coat is shown here in a simple brown homespun cloth. The shirt collar is buttoned instead of open as in Figure 126.

Many men had to wear these clothes into battle, especially during the early years of the Revolution; so they are shown here with the military shoulder straps, pouch, and tricorne hat. This is the outfit traditionally associated with the Minutemen.

Men of all ages, and young boys too, wore the open waistcoat like this in a variety of fabrics from brocade to homespun.

Plate 3

Plate 4

Statesmen or businessmen wore the cutaway coat of Figure 124 in a variety of fabrics. This daytime version has a small collar which sometimes was just the high neck turned down.

The front edges are bound with the same green cloth as the coat, perhaps in imitation of the turned-back military lapels.

Buttons might be steel, pearl, or cloth-covered to match the coat. The cuff buttons are used vertically along the slit instead of horizontally across the cuffs as in former years.

Sometimes daytime knee breeches were made of buff-colored leather as shown instead of cloth matching the coat.

The hunting shirt of Figure 129 is worn on the outside of the breeches and belted. Usually these shirts were linen but occasionally deerskin. Linen ones might be dyed brown, blue, green, purple, or left natural like this one. It is worn over Indian breeches which have a flap down the outside of the leg like those of Figure 174. These leggings with flaps were not commonly worn until early 19th century but during the late 18th century some men deep in the wilderness adopted the Indian style.

Plate 5

Plate 6

The American Continental infantry uniform of Figure 148 is worn with the long buff trousers ordered in 1778 and the crossed shoulder straps for holding cartridge pouch, bayonet, and tomahawk. (The powder horn was on its own strap or hung from the bed roll along with the canteen.)

Coats were blue or brown with lapels of white, red, buff, or blue depending on which colony was represented. This uniform has the buff facings and white lining of New Jersey and New York troops.

This also was the uniform worn by Washington's guards. General Washington is shown in portraits both in the officer version of this one and with the red facings of the Virginia Militia.

The American Continental artillery uniform of blue coat and red lapels with white bound buttonholes was officially adopted in 1779. (Sometimes the buttonhole braid is shown as yellow.)

Enlisted men wore gaiters or spatterdashes of black or buff in several different lengths but these short black ones are most often pictured in historical accounts.

Officers wore boots, sashes, and epaulettes as shown in Figure 149.

Plate 7

Plate 8

The drop-shouldered shirt illustrated in Figure 126 was sometimes worn on the outside of the breeches and belted as shown here.

Wherever white men and Indians came in close contact with each other they tended to dress more like each other. The Indian agent of Figure 160 probably wore deerskin leggings when in the forest as this man does.

One Mohawk chief was portrayed as early as 1710 wearing a white man's white shirt with bare legs and moccasins turned up as in Figure 81.

As white men wore Indian leggings over their knee breeches and the Indian adopted the shirt they both looked much like this man at times.

The dress of Figure 106 with only minor changes was worn throughout much of the 18th century in America by many different classes of women. Well-to-do women, rural women of both England and colonial America as well as servants and slaves wore some version of it. The main difference among the groups was in the type of cloth used, which varied from silks, to homespuns to cheap calicos.

Here the skirt is split in front and drawn up in back to form panniers on each side showing the petticoat underneath. Aprons were worn either over the skirt or underneath and over the petticoat as shown.

The bonnet grew in size toward the end of the century.

Plate 9

The dresses of Figures 132 through 136 have many lovely variations such as this one from an old fashion print. This one is slightly shorter—about two inches above the floor.

A lace-edged kerchief is worn wide and tucked inside the bodice over the chemise.

Aprons were elegant fashion as well as for work during the 18th century; so this one of pink silk was more for looks than for protection.

The low-crowned hat of Figure 105 continued to be worn in the American colonies for many years, growing larger and stiffer toward the end of the century. This one is made of linen covered with crewel embroidery and worn over a small, close-fitting bonnet.

Plate 10

The round neckline, plain skirt, and shirred sleeves of Figure 133 are shown here in another variation. These sleeves have several small rows of shirred white cloth, either silk or sheer muslin, the only decoration on the dress.

No kerchief is needed because the chemise is pulled up to fill in the neckline. The bodice has hooks down the front concealed by a panel.

An unusual bonnet shown in one folk portrait is plain with no fullness and is worn over the tall wig like a pillow case. It is edged with lace around the opening and along the seam over the top of the head. Crewel embroidery decorates the front. It has a point in front forming a heart shape around the face.

Plate 11

The long, loose robes of Figures 87 and 88 continued to be worn during most of the 18th century in many lengths, becoming smaller in the 1770s and 80s as shown in Figures 134 and 152. Although the dresses underneath changed and the bonnets grew in size, the robes changed very little.

They were always worn casually, even off the shoulders at times. Some portraits show them all the way off the shoulders down to the bend of the arms, appearing at first glance more like a stole than a robe. One fashion print showed a long robe worn in this manner trailing on the floor for several inches in back.

Plate 12

Riding habits and walking dresses of the 1780s and 90s sometimes had kerchiefs so puffed out in front that women were said to resemble pigeons from the side. This striped taffeta dress, like that shown in Figure 154, has a kerchief several yards long. It comes around the shoulders loosely, is tied with a ribbon in front (it does not cross), and is secured to the dress. It then goes to the back, where it is fastened or tied, forming a bustle.

The wide-brimmed hat is trimmed with gauze and ribbons. It was fashionable to curl the hat or bonnet ribbons, possibly in imitation of the long curls which hung from under the wigs and frizzed hair.

One fashion print of the period showed a dress almost identical to this one except for the sleeves, which were like those of Figure 169.

1750-1800

Figure 120

(Worn until the end of the 18th century.) This woman, probably rural, older, or just conservative, wears another variation of the kerchief. Her dress has cuffed sleeves over the chemise ruffles and a divided skirt over a petticoat.

The large triangular kerchief is spread over the shoulders and upper arms like a shawl. It is secured by the apron strings which go around to the back, cross, and go around again. Then the ends of the kerchief, hanging down at this point, are puffed up and tucked down into the apron leaving two puffs as shown. They are arranged carefully and artistically so that they fan out prettily. English farmers' wives wore kerchiefs this way.

She wears mitts and a ruffled bonnet which ties under the chin.

Older women loved to wear dark satin dresses with a sheer white kerchief, apron, and lace ruffles on the sleeves. Old ladies liked black satin.

Figure 121

(Worn through the 1780s) This full flowing dress of the 60s is much like Figure 96 but the back fullness has moved inward toward the center. The dress of former years had the fullness all the way to the armhole. One side-view portrait of this period shows that the bodice is fitted close to the body to the center back where it meets the other side, then folds back toward the sides, then is pleated several times before returning to the center. When you have on a full robe and you run your hands from the side seam toward the back and push all the fullness out behind, you produce the same effect. If this fullness is then flattened against the upper back (with the help of someone else), the result can help to give some understanding of the structure of this dress.

This style was worn until after the American Revolution.

Yellow silk flowered cloth was used for one dress like this. Taffetas and silk brocades in pastels were especially popular as well as India cottons.

The hair styles worn with this dress in the 60s were small and lightly powdered. In the 70s they grew higher and more heavily powdered and were decorated with combs and plumes.

89

Figure 122

Little boys had to wear skirts until they were out of diapers and completely dry. Usually they wore coats like men over skirts instead of breeches but sometimes they wore dresses that looked quite feminine.

The first little boy wears a low-necked bodice which has sleeves with wide cuffs. The cuffs have little button tabs on them. The same silver buttons are used on the front.

The skirt is divided over a petticoat but both are flared rather than gathered as was the custom for boys. A wide sash goes around the waist under the bodice and ties in front. His shoes are buckled over the instep. His hair is worn with rolls over the ears and a ribbon in the back which comes to the front and ties around the neck.

In the center, another young boy wears a coat of "old fashioned" design. It has shoulder tabs and slashed sleeves with lace cuffs. The shirt sleeves show through the slashes. The front and pockets of this pastel satin suit are trimmed with braid. His knee breeches match the coat.

He wears white stockings and dark shoes. His hat is a tricorne with gold braid and plumes.

On the right a servant boy wears a coat of yellow with black braid, black collar and cuffs. It is stylishly cutaway at the sides. When the carriage becomes commonly used this black braid will be identified with adult livery. For now, it is becoming more and more associated with servants of all ages.

The waistcoat and breeches are yellow, the shoes and stockings black. His hat, when he wears one, is a black tricorne with matching braid. Adults wear this same outfit.

CHAPTER 5

"Shaggy Hunters" and Clothes of Your Own Spinning

1770 to 1790

1770s Before and During the Revolution

In 1772 merchants in Providence, Rhode Island, burned the British schooner Gaspee. Some of these same merchants later fought alongside the ships of the new Continental Navy which had only forty deep-water ships and a few small boats on the Great Lakes. At the end of the Revolution only three of these were left but America had proven to the world that she had a navy. Abraham Whipple who was one of those privateers captured ten British ships in ten successive nights!

Although there were no official uniforms the privateers did dress in the formal clothes of military officers. This commander wears a dark blue coat which has cuffs but no collar. The turned-back lapels and cuffs are red. Most of these coats had no braid trim but some had braid edging the lapels and cuffs as shown.

The red waistcoats were almost always gold-embroidered and sometimes edged with gold braid as well.

The shirt is like that of Figure 73. The breeches are dark blue like the coat but have gold embroidery around the knee band.

His stockings are white, his buckled shoes and tricorne hat are black. Sometimes the hats were edged with gold braid.

Some privateer captains wore a white or buff waistcoat and lapels instead of red. The waistcoat always had a great deal of braid.

John Paul Jones' portrait shows him in the same uniform of navy blue coat with red lapels and waistcoat, epaulettes, and a tricorne edged with fringe. Instead of a cockade his tricorne has an embroidered medallion.

Figure 123

Figure 124

(Worn through the 80s) The second Continental Congress met at Philadelphia in 1775 in violation of English laws and was therefore revolutionary! There were important jobs to be done by civilian statesmen as well as by military men. Civilian men's clothing was still much like that of Figures 110 and 111.

Most of the signers of the Declaration of Independence were dressed in clothes of the finest quality and along fashionable lines. Their attitude seemed to be, judging from their own writings, that men of standing have a duty to dress tastefully in order to win the respect of other men while at the same time winning respect for the nation as a whole in the eyes of other nations—especially England.

The designers of the Constitution of 1787 also wore a suit like Figure 124 in a variety of fabrics from homespun to velvet. Most of the men involved wore this style and that of Figure 146 into old age because they never adopted the new long trousers. They wore coats of newer designs in later years but accepting the new pantaloons was difficult for most men after a certain age.

This coat was worn by fashionable men. The front corners are rounded back almost to the side seam or cut-away. It is still split in back. It has no collar but the neckline is curved up onto the neck to almost cover the shirt collar. It has frog closings with little tassels but buttons were used on many coats, too. There are no cuffs but the sleeves are split for several inches at the back seam. These splits were rarely buttoned so the fullness of the shirt sleeve shows through.

The light-colored waistcoat has become quite short, up to where the thighs join the hips. It is trimmed with embroidery on the edges and pocket flaps.

The breeches match the waistcoat even to the embroidery around the buckled knee band.

He wears white stockings and black shoes with silver buckles. His hair is powdered, or a wig, and tied back with a black ribbon. The front hair is in short, slightly frizzed bangs.

A New England businessman was described at this time as wearing a pea-green coat, buff breeches with white vest and stockings. His shoe buckles, "covered at least half the foot from instep to toe."

92

Dressing gowns were extremely popular with gentlemen of all ages. Many famous statesmen, including Benjamin Franklin, wore them for their portraits. These gowns, called banyans, were intended for wear at home while relaxing or entertaining but were even seen on the streets in the morning sometimes. They are pictured in the dining rooms of inns also.

This dressing gown of brocade has the neckline turned back into lapels and huge cuffs at the wrists. It probably is reversible as many of them were at this time.

These gowns were almost always worn over the breeches, waistcoat, shirt, and cravat. (One famous portrait shows the neck of the shirt open and no cravat.) A few buttons of the waistcoat were opened for ventilation.

This gentleman wears one stocking loose to show how some of them were held up. They are known to have been buttoned into a breeches button but a painting of men eating at an inn shows a stocking like this one with a button loop.

His shoes are the informal pantofles. They have no back and the instep comes up high on the foot. These shoes appeared out of doors in several drawings; they are not just bedroom slippers.

His cap, a tam-o'-shanter, was worn when the wig was removed. Men sometimes wore these caps during dinner. The lace cap of Figure 64 was still worn too.

One portrait of Ben Franklin shows him in a blue brocade gown with orange lapels like this; in one mezzotint his gown is fur-trimmed and worn with a fur cap.

John Hancock was seen, at noon, in "a red velvet cap within which was one of fine linen, the last turned up two or three inches over the lower edge of the velvet." He wore "a blue damask gown lined with velvet, a white cravat, a white satin embroidered waistcoat, black satin small-clothes [breeches], white silk stockings and red morocco slippers."

This dressing gown was worn by military officers, too.

Figure 125

(Worn throughout the 18th century) This man gives a more accurate idea of the everyday wear for most young men and working men. Paul Revere's portrait by John Singleton Copley shows him dressed this way.

His dark waistcoat is unbuttoned. His breeches and stockings are dark, his buckled shoes black.

His shirt still has the dropped shoulder line that was common until beyond mid-19th century. He wears the neckline open. The portrait of Revere, like some others, shows the cuff button unfastened also. A bit of cloth shows inside his sleeve opening and appears to be the ruffle which he has turned inside. This idea can be used in theatre costuming to great advantage. The same shirt can be worn in one scene with the ruffle showing and in another with it tucked inside.

This man's natural hair is combed straight back on top and down on the sides. It is caught in back with a black bow.

These simple clothes were of homespun cloth in dark colors such as black, brown, gray, or dull green.

Sometimes the collar was worn closed with a cravat even without the coat. The cravat is first held with the center of it at the front of the neck. Both ends are then wound around to the back where they cross and continue on to the front where the ends are tied. When the shirt has a frill as in Figure 73, the tied ends just blend in with the frill.

When a plain shirt without a frill is worn with the cravat, the knot of the cravat is worn in the back.

The apron of Figure 109 was often worn with these clothes.

Men wore no body linen or undershorts but they really were not needed because these shirts come down to almost mid-thigh.

Figure 126

Early American Costume

This outfit appears in more than one crowd or riot scene. In one political cartoon the men are labelled "ruffians." This short jacket which has appeared throughout history (Figures 6, 94, and 103) has changed very little with time.

The jacket, often blue or green, is worn with the petticoat breeches of Figure 61 *over* contemporary knee breeches instead of the bloomer-type breeches formerly worn underneath.

His red hat is as timeless as his jacket, having appeared with little change through the centuries.

More than 30,000 Scotch and Irish immigrants came to the colonies between 1771 and 1773. Most of them were farmers and textile workers. This man could be one of these wearing a jacket over his smock (see Figure 128). European sailors sometimes wore petticoat breeches, too.

In Benjamin West's famous painting, *Penn's Treaty with the Indians,* (1771) young men wear the petticoat breeches with the shirt and vest of Figure 126.

The Boston "massacre" of 1770 was not really a massacre but it was enough of a skirmish or riot between soldiers and townspeople so that five colonists were killed. Henry Pelham's engraving of the incident (copied by Paul Revere) shows the townsmen clad in coats of former years such as those of Figures 92 and 101, but one man wears the short jacket and pantaloons of Figure 103.

Figure 127

Figure 128

(Worn as late as the Civil War.) Farmers and factory workers throughout Europe have worn the smock for many years. Early writings and pictures attest to this and to the fact that smocks were worn in colonial America (and on up to the Civil War).

Some of the early battles were fought along roadsides and in fields. Farmers literally dropped their farm implements, grabbed their muskets and powder horns, and joined in to defend their homes. When the fighting was over they went back to their farm tasks. Continental soldiers were not professional, their interests were local and they were led by local officers for the most part. Few men could take part in the fighting over a long period of time.

This farmer wears a smock with the decorative embroidery stitch which takes its name from the garment—smocking. It has a wide neck and a large collar filled in with the neckerchief that workers have always worn.

These knee breeches and the striped stockings were common at this time. Some hose were horizontally striped. This man wears short gaiters or leggings over his black shoes and the wide-brimmed hat so loved by Englishmen.

English farmers liked green or unbleached smocks or unbleached ones with green trim; Germans preferred black ones, and factory workers generally liked blue ones although this is not a hard, fast rule.

The blue factory smocks of Europe evolved into the blue or gray uniforms and shirts worn by delivery men, drivers, repair men, etc., of the 20th century, resulting in the term "blue collar worker."

The main uniforms during the early years of the war were the smocks and hunting clothes and whatever men happened to be wearing when drawn into the fight although a few militia companies had their own uniforms.

About two weeks after George Washington was made commander of the American army he rode to Cambridge, in Massachusetts Bay Colony, to take charge of the 16,000 men waiting there. Congress sent him 3,000 more from the middle colonies. Since there were no uniforms to issue, he requested that they wear their hunting shirts "to unite the men and abolish those provincial distinctions." He reportedly commented on the psychological aspects of these shirts, saying that professional soldiers always assumed that anyone wearing hunting clothes was a sharpshooter!

The English made many snobbish references to the colonial soldiers using such terms as "shaggy hunters" and "rabble" and "homespuns." Whether it was the psychological advantage already mentioned or not, it is a fact that the English spent a lot of time writing and talking about the Americans' hunting clothes.

This soldier wears a linen hunting shirt with two fringe-trimmed collars for extra protection during wet or cold weather. One collar covers the shoulders, the other is smaller. Fringe covers the seams which were numerous as every piece of precious handwoven cloth was utilized. It also helps drain off water by allowing it to break up into droplets and drip off the fringe instead of going into the seams. The cuffs have pleated linen ruffles instead of fringe.

Fringe was often dyed blue or green, perhaps a carryover of the English custom of using green trim on their smocks (as mentioned in Figure 128).

When worn on the outside of the breeches the shirt was sometimes belted as in Color plate No. 4.

Figure 129

Figure 130

This is the hunting shirt or smock as sketched by a German eyewitness in 1775. It has much fringe and is rather long but some were even longer than this.

Often the knee breeches were worn with Indian leggings protecting the lower leg. The leggings of southern marksmen are described as made of coarse woolen cloth, tied with garters and coming to mid-way on the thighs. The same description mentions moccasins and leather Indian breeches on some of them (see Figures 34 and 81).

In October of 1776 General Washington asked Congress for hunting shirts and "Indian boots instead of stockings," to protect the legs from briers. Washington advised each colony to equip its own troops in hunting shirts or smocks. In spite of an order of 1775 by Congress that all the army should wear brown many regiments dyed their hunting shirts green, blue, black, or purple.

A few hunting coats were just leather copies of fashionable coats. One museum example known to have been made by Indians is embellished with quillwork designs but is cut on lines like that of Figure 124 and is quite beautiful.

Their hats were either homemade versions of the grenadier cap (Figures 86 and 117-left) or tricornes "burnt by the sun till a redish hue."

Early American Costume

Women defied King George III even before their husbands did. The King, in order to help his weavers' guilds at home, decreed that though American women might raise flax and wool, make it into thread and dye it, they might not weave it! Even when the weaving equipment that her husband had made was sitting in her own house she was not to weave her own cloth for her own family's clothes! Women did weave and in doing so defied the strict laws that said they must send the yarn to England for someone else to weave and then buy the cloth. Women said that the first drumbeat of the revolution was the "bump bump" of their weaving looms.

But not all the women were weaving their own cloth. Many were still buying imported cloth and dresses too, especially silk. They would continue to wear the dresses they already had, too.

This dress of green, rose, gold, pink, and beige floral silk is quite elegant with its predominant green color. The bodice is worn over a corset of the same cloth which shows in the front. The bodice hooks together at the point and probably has some concealed hooks higher up.

The elbow-length sleeves have a pleated cuff which curves to fit the bend of the arm. The chemise ruffles show above the corset and at the sleeves. This corset fastens in the back (see Figure 107). Sometimes the corset and bodice were the same and might fasten in back or front.

The skirt is divided over a white petticoat.

The lady wears the "creped" and powdered hair. It is curled tightly with a curling iron and then "creped" or teased until it stands quite high and can be shaped in any one of a number of popular designs. Some of these hair styles use the natural hair, some are wigs, and most are a combination of natural hair plus some false hair. (See Figure 166 for hair bolster.)

Figure 131

(Worn through the 80s.) Many women in the larger towns along the coast dressed elegantly, even extravagantly. Many were loyalists who entertained the beautifully uniformed and equipped British soldiers at parties and balls in the early 70s before the war.

In 1776, 60,000 loyalists or Tories left the colonies because they feared a social revolution as well as a political one. Most of them were landowners, officeholders, and families of the military.

But in 1778 France joined the war on America's side. Later when the French army arrived, the ladies who were patriots or Whigs entertained in their turn the dashing young Frenchmen. Where there were armies, especially officers, there were lovely young ladies and military balls. Where there were young ladies and military balls, there were beautiful ball gowns.

This lovely ball gown is made much like Figure 131 but has front closings instead of the deep "V" opening. The pastel silk dress is trimmed with ruchings of the same fabric. Ruchings are ruffles which are stitched and gathered or pleated down the middle so that there is a ruffle on both edges—a double ruffle. They trim the neck, the bodice, the sleeves, the front of the skirt opening, and the petticoat. This dress is simple compared to many which had the ruchings put on in scallops, circles, swirls, zigzags, and rows of varying widths. This lady even wears a ruching around her neck.

Gauze (similar to tulle) is used on the dresses in swags and puffs and drapes also. The lady's high powdered hair is topped with a turban of gauze caught in swags across her head. She also wears a plume.

Figure 132

Figure 133

This young lady wears a pale blue satin dress w[...]
neckline of lace. The lace which is already of a scalloped[...]
in each curve with a ribbon and pulled in a bit more. [...]
has concealed hooks under the front panels or it hook[...]
back (see Figure 107 for undergarments). The sleeves [...]
inches of shirring with a little heading on the sleeves and[...]
lace and satin ruffles at the elbow. These ruffles are dee[...]
on top of the arm so they hang beautifully.

The skirt is plain satin to match the bodice. She we[...]
crewel embroidered apron over the point of the bodice[...]
gold lace.

Women of the colonies were called "lazy squaws[...]
women because they sat for hours embroidering instead[...]
and working in the fields! Almost every town had at le[...]
gave needlework lessons. Some men schoolmasters [...]
broidery, feather work, and purse and handkerchief n[...]

Her necklace is three strands of pearls. Her hair is [...]
blue ribbon and decorated on top with ribbon bows an[...]

This dress can be adapted to any age from youth [...]
aging matrons.

(Worn through the 80s.) Striped or floral taffetas and linens as well
as satins and India cottons were used for these dresses with jackets or
"caracos." The jackets varied in length from full-length to short like this
one. The fur-trimmed coat (right) falls about to the knees. Coats were
usually so wide apart in front that they did not come together at all.

The corset-bodice of matching fabric is worn over the chemise and
skirt. The corset fastens with hook and eyes under the ruche. (For
undergarments, see Figure 107.) The jacket was usually, but not always,
of the same fabric as the bodice and skirt. They were all decorated with
self ruchings and bows. (See Figure 132 for ruchings.) The neckline is
filled in with a soft kerchief.

The lady's bonnet, with ruchings also, sits on her high hair style. It
has a large bow in back.

The winter coat with fur trim (right) is a variation of the same jacket.
She wears the dress jacket under the coat. She wears gloves and carries a
muff of the same fur. These muffs often had a large ribbon bow on them.

Her bonnet is large, though not as large as some. The ruffles get
smaller toward the top so that they come to a point.

A full-length version of this jacket appears on the mother in the book
jacket painting.

Early American Costume

When Bostonians decided to boycott British goods before the war, British cloth was one of the main targets. Young militants even wrote a song about loving the ladies who were dressed in clothes of their "own make and spinning."

This dress in dull brown fabric over a petticoat of brown-and-white stripe has the look of homespun cloth.

The patriotic young woman in one folk portrait could probably well afford silks and brocades instead of this dull brown. Perhaps her husband (shown in a matching portrait) was one of the privateer captains mentioned in Figure 123. The portrait is labelled *Captain*. If so, then her dull dress must certainly be of her own make and spinning.

The plain brown bodice fastens in back with hooks or laces. It has the pleated cuffs which conform to the bend of the arm. Her white chemise sleeve ruffles, and possibly an extra one or two, show below the cuffs. She wears a sheer, triangular white kerchief around her neck and shoulders; it is delicately embroidered. A large salmon-colored bow holds it in place. The cuffs have bows of the same color. All three ribbons are pinked on the ends and the two on the sleeves are tied in half-bows with only one loop.

The full skirt is bordered down the front with peaked strips of the brown-and-white striped cloth used for the petticoat. These borders with their peaks are used on the petticoat too.

Her bonnet, large as it is, is smaller than some of the period. The ruffle is turned so that it goes up onto the bonnet instead of down around the face as in Figure 134. It has a salmon ribbon bow with the streamer ends going over the bonnet and down the back a way. Lace lappets hang down in back as in Figure 76, only shorter.

She wears a bead necklace and dark lace mitts. She holds a fan.

irl's dress
eves and
wn each

a ribbon
n rosette
ruffles of

Figure 136

98

Young boys dressed like their fathers in collarless coats with the front corners curved toward the back. The very large buttons on this coat appear to be covered in crochet or cloth.

His shirt has a neck frill and small ruffles on the wristbands.

The waistcoat is of a wide striped fabric with the stripes running horizontally.

The same light color is used for both the breeches and coat. The stockings are white. His hair is lightly powdered, pulled back and tied with a black ribbon with one roll over each ear.

Figure 137

Figure 138

(Worn into early 19th century.) A little girl wears a muslin or gauze dress of white with a pink ribbon sash. It has ruffles around the neck and elbow-length sleeves.

A narrow strip of pink ribbon is tied around her sleeves and around her hair like a headband.

A little boy wears a velvet suit with pantaloons which have a front flap shown more clearly on Figure 183.

His jacket is double-breasted. A wide satin sash is worn around the waist and tied in back without streamers. The blouse has a wide lace collar. A similar blouse can be seen without the jacket in Figure 212.

His stockings are white, his buckled shoes are blue. A plume adorns his hat.

99

Shirring on the sleeves was so popular that it was used on even the tiniest dress. This little girl wears a simple dress of a soft tan color with a sash of brown satin. The bodice has a lace front with a center panel of shirring and lace around the neck. The dress is ankle-length and she wears red shoes. Red shoes were worn more and more by babies and young children at this time.

The baby wears a similar dress. Its sleeves have a shirred cuff with a tiny ruffle. The wide neck is edged with a narrow lace. The floor-length skirt has several rows of tucks around it just above the hem.

The hat is a dark color with a plume.

There was a desperate shortage of pins in the colonies during the Revolution but of course baby diapers were tied, not pinned.

Figure 139

Figure 140

1770s - 1780s "The Other Side"

A loyalist Highlander regiment was recruited in the colonies as one of eleven loyalist companies.

In the years 1776 and 1777 they wore the uniforms which were designed during the Scottish rebellion of 1745. (At that time the Scots were put down by the British and many were sent to America as punishment.)

The red coat with buff cuffs is quite short. It has a small collar, worn open to show the shirt and black cravat tied in back. Braided cords are looped on his right shoulder.

He wears the traditional plaid kilt which is straight in front and pleated at the sides and back.

The shoulder plaid is fastened to his left shoulder and tucked into his belt under his right arm.

His shoulder strap, belt, cartridge pouch, and shoes are all black. The sporran or pouch in front below the belt is a kind of purse needed because the kilt has no pockets.

His stockings are red and white plaid of an ancient design. They are gartered with ribbons and bows. His black tam-o'-shanter has a bow on the front and a pompon on top. He carries a sword, musket, and a pistol.

100

The Highlander's kilts of Figure 140 were discontinued in 1778 in favor of trousers. (The beloved traditional kilts were revived early in the 19th century and continued to be worn into the 20th century.)

The regiments were issued buff trousers designed after the Indian legging and combined with breeches. They have a very practical leather patch on the knees and straps under the shoes.

The red jacket with very short tails with white linings buttoned back also has black cuffs, collar, and lapels. The leather elbow patches are black. He wears a short buff waistcoat.

His Highlander cap is black with a red and white plaid band and a red pompon on top.

He carries a gray blanket roll from which hangs a powder horn. He wears crossed black shoulder straps like those shown more clearly in Figure 114. They hold his canteen, bayonet, tomahawk, and pouch.

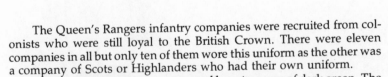

Figure 141

The Queen's Rangers infantry companies were recruited from colonists who were still loyal to the British Crown. There were eleven companies in all but only ten of them wore this uniform as the other was a company of Scots or Highlanders who had their own uniform.

The Rangers wore coats, vests, and long trousers of dark green. The lapels buttoned back with steel buttons but they were the same green as the coat. The tails of the coat were lined with white which showed when the tails were fastened back.

The long trousers of the British North American Light Infantry of the 1750s were retained (see Figure 114), but made more close fitting.

The shirt had a frill at the front opening and on the wristband.

The tall black hat had a cloth stocking cap top of green with a tassel and decorated with a silver crescent. His short, pointed-top boots and the shoulder strap were black.

There was a trend toward more functional military uniforms and the British often set the styles for the rest of the world. It was many years before camouflage was used in uniforms to any degree even though they used the green because of past experiences in the American forests.

Figure 142

Here is the British Infantry uniform of the period: red coats with black lapels, collar, and cuffs; buttonholes bound in white and brass buttons. The coattail corners are lined with white.

The waistcoat, knee breeches, and stockings are white. They were sometimes buff.

Enlisted men wore either the tricorne or regular grenadier hat of Figure 117. The hair has a roll over each ear and a pigtail braid in back.

The gaiters or leggings are black and worn over black shoes. They come to a point in the back like those of the American soldier of Figure 148.

He wears a black cravat over the collar of his shirt. His belt is white as are the straps which hold the backpack. The backpack or bed roll was sometimes covered with goatskin.

He wears two white shoulder straps like those of the French soldier of Figure 151 (omitted here so that the coat lapels and bed roll straps can be seen).

Figure 143

German or Hessian soldiers were hired by the British to help fight the American colonists. They were called Hessians because most of them were hired in Hesse-Kassel and Hesse-Hanau, Germany.

They wore dark green coats with fancy white braiding on the red lapels. Each buttonhole has a tassel at the edge of the lapel. Two of these braid designs with tassels were sewn on each sleeve and two more on each side below the lapel. White braid designs on the shoulders and upper sleeves also probably indicated officers. The cuffs and coattail lining were red.

This Hessian wears buff waistcoat and knee breeches. His black gaiters come up almost to mid-thigh. They are worn over black shoes.

His white shirt has a black cravat around the collar which ties around his powdered hair in back. He wears a tall black fur hat with an embroidered plate in front.

His shoulder strap is white with a large black pouch. It is not shown, so that the braided buttonholes and lapels can be clearly seen.

Some records show the coats dark blue and one is blue-green. Some show yellow vests.

Figure 144

1770s - 1780s During and After the Revolution

A fascinating combination of Indian and gentlemen's clothing! The red coat is double-breasted and can have the buff lapels folded back and buttoned to its own side like military coats. There are numerous portraits of such clothes worn by men who worked or lived with the Indians. One has a leather sash with fringed ends wrapped around the waist and tied. It is worn under the coat, over the vest.

The Indian blanket was traditionally worn like a cloak over the left shoulder, under the right arm, and tied in front. It is shown over the arms here in order to show the clothing underneath. It is red, tan, brown, and black.

He wears Indian moccasins and snug-fitting deerskin leggings drawn up over the buff breeches. They are gartered at the knees with Indian quillwork garters.

Quillwork decoration is used on the black cap as well as feathers. This hat is an Indian-made version of the grenadier cap of the British Army during the Seven Years War. (It was originally worn by Austrian, Prussian, and Hessian armies earlier in the century and had a metal plate in front.) Other homemade versions of the grenadier cap were worn by some of the Continental Army regiments early in the Revolution (see Figure 130).

His cravat is black and tied once, then tucked into the vest.

Scotch and Irish traders who were "friend and brother" to the Indians roamed and worked over a 2,000-mile area in what is now Kentucky and Tennessee in the 1740s. Sir William Johnson had worked with Indians in the Mohawk Valley as early as 1738.

This costume and that of Figure 160 are used mainly to demonstrate how clothing which follows the trends of the time is adapted to certain needs and takes on a special character in doing this. These clothes are unique because of their particular combination of items of clothing from more than one way of dressing and living.

Figure 145

Figure 146

(Worn during 80s and 90s) The Constitutional Convention of 1787 was composed of men ranging in age from 26 to 81 so the representatives wore a variety of clothing. Benjamin Franklin still held to the large cuffs and full skirts of Figure 101. Most of the men have been pictured wearing clothes shown in Figures 110 and 111. The more fashionable ones wear the suits of Figure 124 and this one, 146.

President George Washington chose for his inauguration in 1789 a simple brown suit, woven of 100 percent American homespun. He wished to show, by not appearing in uniform, that America was a government of the people and not of the military. (For officials' robes see Figure 102.)

Figure 146 shows a coat with back splits that can be worn either single-breasted with the lapels buttoned back or lapped over in double-breasted fashion. Some gentlemen, like this one, wore the coat casually with none of the buttons used for either fashion. Occasionally, the lapels were a lighter color than the coat. It had no cuffs, just the fashionable buttoned splits which revealed the shirt sleeve ruffle and were often left open. Buttons were cloth-covered or steel.

The double-breasted vest is made of brocade. It is turned back with lapels at the chest and shows the frill of the shirt opening (see Figure 73).

The breeches are calf-length so that they go down into the boots. Buttons go up the leg several inches.

Boots are the English style with the tops turned down to show the canvas lining. He wears spurs. His boots have boot straps because they are quite snug. Shoes and stockings like those of Figure 124 were still worn.

The hair is natural and worn in one roll over each ear with the back tied in a ribbon. The tricorne hat remains in style.

In Edward Savage's painting of *The Washington Family* (1789-96) Washington wears this suit. His favorite servant, Billy Lee, wears one almost identical but in a lighter color than Washington's.

Early American Costume

One contemporary sketch of a riot (a farmers' rebellion of 1786) shows several men wearing this shirt, vest, and knee breeches with vertically striped stockings. This man's hat is the large flat hat traditionally favored by farmers. Others in the group who also wear the striped stockings have their hats folded up into tricornes. His costume is typical of the clothing worn by farmers at this time.

His hair is all pulled back and tied with a dark string. His black shoes have large buckles. Blue-and-white vertically striped stockings were worn from the 1770s to 1810. Sometimes they were horizontally striped. The dress of another protestor or rioter a few years earlier is shown in Figure 127.

Figure 147

In 1775 Congress decided that the American army should wear brown because that was the dye easiest to obtain locally. Such orders as "Shirts and breeches made of tow-cloth steeped in a tan-vat till the color of a dry leaf" resulted in many shades of brown since the men furnished their own.

The only uniforms at the time were for a few groups of militia and those of Washington and his guards who wore blue coats with buff lapels and breeches. Even those militiamen who wore uniforms when they joined the fight soon found them worn and tattered. The choice, then, was to use hunting clothes when the militia uniform was worn out or to wear the hunting clothes in camp and in battle and save the uniform for dress wear.

Many paintings show the calf-high gaiters with a peak in the back (left) during much of the war. In 1778 it was decided that long buff trousers with a strap under the foot should be worn (right).

Most of the leather straps, belts, and pouches of the Americans had been taken as booty during early battles.

The Light Infantry Corps, an honor group selected from various regiments, was formed in 1777. In 1780 each man in the corps was presented with a billed, hard leather cap (left). It had a bear fur crest and red and black plumes.

In order to distinguish officers, Washington decreed that Generals and staff officers would wear baldrics over their vests, under their coats; Captains would wear yellow cockades on their hats, with Lieutenants wearing green and field officers red.

Some records show that the *infantry* from different colonies wore different color lapels even after an order of 1779 for uniformity. Massachusetts, Connecticut, New Hampshire, and Rhode Island used white facings; Delaware, Virginia, Pennsylvania, and Maryland, red facings; New Jersey and New York buff facings. Georgia and the Carolinas wore blue facings with buttonholes bound in white as in Figure 149.

148

104

In 1778 the Massachusetts *artillery* regiment was equipped in new uniforms of blue coats with a white lining and red lapels and cuffs. Vests and long trousers were white.

In 1779 this Massachusetts uniform was adopted as the model for the uniform of the American *artillery* throughout the colonies with but one change. The white lining which shows at the coattails would be red to match the lapels and cuffs. These uniforms were purchased in France.

This official American Continental Artillery uniform consists of a coat of dark blue with red lapel facings, lining, and cuffs. The buttonhole facings are yellow and the buttons brass.

The vest and breeches are white, his cravat is black. Sometimes the cravat and hair ribbon are one and the same. It goes around the neck, ties, then ties around the hair.

This soldier is an officer so he wears the red sash and epaulettes, sword, and black boots of an officer. His hat is the gold-edged tricorne, also of an officer as are the white gloves.

Enlisted men wore gaiters over shoes instead of boots. They wore two white shoulder straps for holding the canteen, tomahawk, pouch, and bayonet and they carried a musket (see Figure 150 for straps).

Figure 149

In 1775 Congress had decreed that brown should be the official color of the American forces so in 1776 when a regiment made up mostly of Canadians was formed, they adopted brown coats with white lapel facings, cuffs, and lining.

The vest, knee breeches, and stockings were white also. The grenadier hat, shoes, cravat, and short gaiters were black. The two crossed shoulder straps were white.

One epaulette of red was worn by sergeants and one of green by corporals.

When new uniforms were available in 1779 the main change was the addition of new red collars, cuffs, lapels, and linings to the brown coats. This made the uniform like the other new ones except that brown replaced the blue.

Figure 150

Early American Costume

France joined the war in 1778. A French army of 5,000 men arrived in Rhode Island in June, 1780, sent by King Louis XVI to help the colonies. They were beautifully equipped and dressed.

For many years the French had had a preference for white uniforms. Their new uniforms were all white except for the trim which might be pale blue, pink, violet, yellow, grey, maroon, orange or green depending on the regiment. One contemporary artist showed them with maroon trim so we will use that color.

On the left an officer wears a white coat with maroon lapels with pearl buttons. It has a stand-up collar. The epaulettes and cuffs are maroon also. The buttons continue after the lapels and cuffs stop so, having a different background, they change to another color. When on white the buttons are maroon. He wears stockings pulled up over his knee breeches and pantofles (see Figure 125). Some pictures show garters just below the knees. The pantofles seem to indicate the officer is off duty at the moment.

On the right a soldier wears the white lapels which are bound on the edges with a narrow maroon binding or braid. The buttons are maroon and continue beyond the lapels and cuffs. The cuffs are maroon as on the other coat.

His gaiters come above the knees. They button all the way up the side. Sometimes garters are worn on these gaiters as on stockings.

Both wear black tricorne hats and black shoes.

One account says that the first order given by their commander after they arrived in America was that they wear a black rosette in the center of the white cockade on their hats as a gesture of friendship. Americans had previously added white centers to their black cockades.

Figure 151

By the end of the 70s dresses were becoming softer, with smaller hoops and no panniers, although some women continued to wear them for a time.

The jacket of Figure 134 is looser and softer now. It is worn over a crewel-embroidered dress of muslin or linen for a daytime dress. It has ruchings around the neck and front and ruffles on the short sleeves.

The newly fashionable dress underneath has long fitted sleeves on a soft bodice without a point. The simple skirt worn over a small hoop and petticoats has only a flounce around the hem. A large sash tied on the left side and a simple ribbon bow at the neck ruffle decorate the dress.

The most outstanding thing about it is the embroidery. It is in blue-greens, salmon-pinks, yellows, browns, soft greens, and dull reds that come from vegetable-dyed, homespun yarns.

Her hair is pulled up in front and put into a topknot. The back hair is softly arranged.

Figure 152

Little girls, as well as adults and older girls, wear the kerchief. This one is pulled up close to the neck, crossed over in front and snugly tied in back to keep it from falling off the shoulder as in Figure 156. The dress is probably muslin. Some children's dresses were already being constructed like that of Figure 182.

Her wide sleeves come to the elbow and are untrimmed. Her skirt is up off the floor a little. Some skirts were several inches above floor-length.

Her bonnet ruffle comes in at the front to expose the ringlet bangs of her hair. It has a pink ribbon.

The baby is dressed in an outfit almost identical. Instead of a kerchief, her (or his) dress has a ribbon sash tied in back; there is a ruffle at the neck, and plain wide sleeves to the elbow.

The bonnet has a ribbon rosette in front. The shoes are red, a color already popular which will become quite common in a few years.

The ribbons on the bonnet and dress may be either pink, blue, or red.

Figure 157

CHAPTER 6

New Clothes for a New Nation

1790 to 1820

Early American Costume

1790s

Figure 158

As westward migrations increased, problems and negotiations with the Indians increased too. In the 70s there had been a treaty with the Cherokees (Figure 81) and trouble with the Shawnees and Delawares (Figure 34). Now that the Revolution was over, the Constitution put to work, and a new President in office, there were other problems to solve as westward travel increased.

Southern farmer or Muskhogean-stock Indians included the Alibamu, Apalachee, Tuskegee, Choctaw, Natchez, Seminole, Muskogee or Creek, and Chickasaw. (Sometimes the stock is called Creek instead of Muskhogean.)

Since these Indians lived where the climate was moderate, they needed very little clothing. Men wore just a long fringe of shredded bark hanging from a belt instead of a breechcloth like the tribes farther north. They added large carved shell ornaments around their necks along with feather necklaces at times. Feather or shredded bark garters were worn in summer. Sometimes woven bracelets adorned the upper arms.

Tobacco was carried in the pouch hanging from a shoulder strap. Another strap held the quiver of his arrows. For special occasions of war, body paint, usually red, was used on the thighs, upper arms, and face.

Indians in all areas of North America always have worn far less in cold weather than the white man could comprehend. If the Muskhogean (Creek) wore any extra clothing in winter it was a cloak made of feathers woven with mulberry bark twine and a pair of leggings of fur or feathers up to just below his knees.

Muskhogean men wore a tuft of hair on top with braids on the sides and a bound tuft from the crown (left). Sometimes, instead of the front tuft of standing hair, there was just a fringe of very short hair across the forehead (right). They greased their hair with bear grease and it was, as a result, very shiny.

Women of the Indian tribes of the Muskhogean stock wore short skirts of shredded bark or Spanish moss or a kilt of deerskin (right). The top of the skirt folded over a woven belt to form a drape.

Their adornments included carved shell disks suspended from leather strips around their necks, and occasionally a necklace, headdress, garters of feathers, and large round earrings.

In cold weather a cloak of woven twined mulberry bark was worn across one shoulder (left). It was occasionally belted.

Women wore their hair long and greased with bear grease. Some of them wore ringlets of hair around the face.

Figure 159

112

Men who worked with the Cherokees and Creeks would be called upon more and more in the coming years to settle disputes as settlers pushed westward across the mountains into Kentucky and Tennessee.

This man's costume is a combination of Indian and fashionable gentleman's clothing. He wears the drop-shouldered, full-sleeved shirt of Figure 73 but with an Indian flavor. The sleeve is puffed out above a bracelet on his right arm. A cloak or blanket is draped over his left shoulder and arm. The neck with its frill on each side of the opening is folded back into lapels. In the open neck he wears a woven Indian band which stands up on its edge and a metal breastplate. These breastplates are crescent-shaped with holes in them for attaching chains or strips of leather. Officers have worn them since the days of armor and so have Indians. Either the Indians saw them on the officers and fashioned some like them, traded for them, or took them from officers killed in battle.

An Indian pouch for tobacco hangs on a strap over his shoulder.

He wears moccasins with his stockings and knee breeches, and probably draws Indian leggings over his breeches when he is in the forest. (See Color plate No. 7)

His hat is a turban trimmed with fur and a woven or beaded band with a medallion in the center at the forehead. There are feathers and plumes on the very top and streamers hang down in back.

When the white man first came the Indians wore little or nothing but as the 19th century approached they took on more and more of the white man's ways including his clothes. Indian chiefs who were painted by artists travelling west wore the white man's shirt with their own traditional clothes. The result was much like this Indian agent's outfit.

Figure 160

Gentlemen still wore knee breeches and many old men would never accept trousers. The French Revolution would help loose trousers or pantaloons to become fashionable.

This gentleman wears a military-style coat for his sporting outfit. It is a dark color with steel buttons. The military lapels are so curved in the cutaway style that they have become purely decorative. It is doubtful if they could even be buttoned double-breasted any more. The coat is held together with two hooks in the center. The stiff stand-up collar and cuffs are decorated with braid.

His shirt has a front frill and his cravat goes all the way around the neck and ties in front. The sleeve ruffles show at the wrists. He wears a buff vest over the shirt.

His buff knee breeches come down onto the leg longer than a few years ago so when boots are worn the knee breeches go down into them. His stockings are white, his black shoes have large silver or steel buckles but little or no tongue in the latest fashion.

The large wide-brimmed hat is worn with the brim flat but the whole hat is cocked to one side.

Figure 161

Early American Costume

Knee breeches were required wear at court in England until the 1830s and as long as that was the case knee breeches would remain fashionable for formal wear.

At one formal gathering given by President and Mrs. Washington the men wore knee breeches with several different styles of coats. Several men representing the clergy and government appeared in the long robes of Figure 102 and most of the women wore dresses like Figures 132, 134, 155, and 164.

This very elegant gentleman wears a cutaway coat of blue velvet with a red lining and elaborate silver embroidery. White embroidery was often used also. This coat has the very fashionable high neck but no collar as formal coats rarely have one. The tails are embroidered on each side of the split.

His shirt has a front frill and wide ruffles fall from the wrists. His cravat is wrapped around twice and tied in a small knot. The red vest is embroidered in silver. The red breeches come down onto the calf a bit with a band of silver embroidery. They are buttoned up the sides.

His stockings are white. His black shoes have buckles but the tongue or front flap is not so large now as shoes are becoming lower.

This is his natural hair (not a wig) pulled back and tied with a black ribbon. The side rolls are lower too, down over the ears.

Figure 162

Figure 163

United States troops wore this uniform as Washington reviewed them in 1794 when they were called in to put down a rebellion by Pennsylvania farmers rioting over a tax on liquor. There were 15,000 militia. (For rioters, see Figure 147.) This same uniform was worn at the Battle of Fallen Timbers in Ohio in 1794 after which the Indians ceded what is now southeastern Indiana and southern Ohio.

The different regiments were distinguished by different colors, but their uniforms were of the same basic cut as the uniform worn by this soldier. The coat has a high stand-up collar and turn-back lapels. It is cut away from the chest, back and down toward the tails which are turned back at the corners.

He wears the new long trousers and riding boots which are higher in front than in back.

The hat is especially important because it is the new bicorne or two-cornered hat, but it is not yet the classic bicorne. It still has a suggestion of a third corner in front and the two points are rather straight as compared to the drooping corners of the bicorne in Figure 175.

Washington and his staff wore dark blue coats with buff lapels and linings. The vest and trousers were buff also. One of his staff had red lapels and white linings, vest, and breeches. Officers wore epaulettes on their shoulders and swords at their sides.

One regiment had light blue coats with white trim and vest and blue trousers. Most regiments wore bright blue coats with red lapels, cuffs, and linings with white vest and breeches.

All enlisted men wore the short gaiters of Figures 148 and 150.

Figure 164

This lady's satin dress has transitional characteristics. It has the new long sleeves which go down onto the hand but the older, pointed bodice.

The kerchief is worn over the shoulders, crossed over the bosom, and then tied or pinned in back. It has a ruffle at the neck either on this kerchief or on another one inside. The kerchief and the large bonnet are very fashionable.

The skirt, also of satin, opens in front and reveals a petticoat with a flounce. Light-colored satins and taffetas were popular for young women while older ladies liked gray or black satin.

The custom of wearing more than one kerchief at a time retained its popularity (see Figure 155).

This woman's dark dress has a natural waistline with no point and sleeves to the elbow with a small ruffle.

She wears, first, a semicircular white kerchief on the outside of the low neck of the dress. It is pinned together in front and anchored to the dress. Over this plain white kerchief she wears a little crescent-shaped black lace one. It is fastened to the white kerchief with a small black bow. The sheer, rounded ends overlap and form a circle design in front. Martha Washington had her portrait painted several times wearing large bonnets and both a white and a black kerchief at the same time. For instance, see Edward Savage's painting, *The Washington Family.*

This bonnet is pulled in and puffed into a tall narrow shape. The satin bows often matched the dresses. A soft blue was popular during this period.

Figure 165

115

Early American Costume

Without a chemise or kerchief the new necklines would completely expose the breasts. They were reported to have been worn that way in France, but those pictured in the United States are modestly filled in.

This neckline can be seen because of the black braid that edges it. The braid continues up alongside the bosom and over the shoulder on a neckline similar to those of Figures 167 and 168, only lower.

The lady's chemise (under the dress bodice) is seen in the "V" of her kerchief. The kerchief comes over the shoulders and falls down on the arms a little, then over the bosom, and is snugly tucked into the bodice. A little sprig of flowers pinned to the kerchief both decorates it and holds it together. The fitted sleeves come to about midway between the elbow and wrist and are edged with lace.

The skirt is plain. She wears a ribbon sash at the waistline of the straight bodice and the popular black cord or narrow ribbon tied high on her neck.

Her hair style is especially noteworthy. It was "crimpted" and "creped" and curled with a hot curling iron to form a mass in the shape of a bonnet. This was formed over a bolster called a "tower" used underneath. This bolster was stuffed with horse hair, cotton, wool, and other materials. Some accounts of these creped hair styles described the hours it took to do them and the headaches that resulted from wearing the heavy tower. The hair was powdered as well as creped.

The long curls that hang down the neck were never creped but appear soft and natural by comparison. The hair tower is decorated with plumes.

Figure 166

The French Revolution caused large numbers of French citizens to flee France in order to escape the guillotine. Many of these new emigrants to America were aristocrats and fashion-conscious people. The French influenced fashions over much of the world but especially in the United States because of our friendship with France during our revolution. French furniture and wall papers were immensely popular too.

This lady's fashionable dress of pastel brocade taffeta has the new low neck and long fitted sleeves. A wide beaded belt or girdle is worn around the waist.

The kerchief is worn in the casual French style. Though it appears casual it still is arranged very precisely. The folds come over the shoulders, then fall wide and puff out in front before being tucked into the chemise and bodice. The chemise can be worn just to fit the neckline or pulled up with its drawstring to fit high as in Figure 166. The kerchief is tucked into the dress and chemise and the ruffle stands up around it. From the side the ruffle and the kerchief puffs give a very bosomy look. French women were discarding the chemise but American women would continue to wear it.

Her necklace is a ribbon worn very high up on the neck with a jeweled pendant and several swags of amber beads. She wears a bracelet with a matching stone.

Her hair is frizzed in a small style with ringlets around her face. It is pulled up in back so that it appears short. She wears a little feather crown with jewels and two large peacock feathers or straight plumes standing up in front.

This dress and that in Figure 166 can both be worn with the chemise pulled up to fill in the neckline as it does in Figures 99 and 181.

Figure 167

A young lady wears a youthful version of the same dress as in Figure 167. It is dull green with a pink sash. Her chemise ruffle is pulled up at the neckline to help fill it in. The chemise ruffles show at the wrists. Although dresses sometimes had lace ruffles sewn right onto them, most American women would continue to wear the chemise for some years.

Her large tan hat worn on the back of her head has dark red plumes. Her hair has soft straight bangs and falls softly on her shoulders in long curls.

Figure 168

Figure 169

This dress, like Figure 167, predicts the new Empire styles to come. It is of soft silk gauze. The bodice is full instead of fitted but it has a fitted lining. The dress is sheer white over a pink satin or taffeta lining. There is a full ruffle with a heading around the neckline. The full gathered sleeves are caught with pink ribbons at the elbow, halfway between the elbow and shoulder, and at the bottom of the sleeve at the lower arm. There probably is a drawstring in each place because every fold is perfectly placed. The sleeves and the bodice are made in much the same way as the little girl's dress of Figure 182.

There was, at this time, an extra sleeve or mitt worn with the new dresses which would be seen more in years to come. It was often like a mitt with openings for the fingers and in some cases like gloves (see also Figure 176). The mitts may match the dress but often they are of white taffeta. Black taffeta ones appear in a number of portraits under pastel dresses.

This lady wears her creped and powdered hair in a broad, squared shape with soft long curls down on her neck and shoulders. She holds her large be-ribboned hat. It is probably straw as straw hat manufacture was started in America in the 1790s.

She wears a black cord tied high around her neck with a miniature portrait hanging from it.

Early American Costume

Soft white muslin was a popular cloth for dresses at this time. This woman's bodice is gathered full at the bosom. The wide pink satin sash is worn slightly above the natural waistline and holds the gathered bodice in under the bosom, predicting the high-waisted Empire gowns soon to come. A large satin rosette bow decorates the sash. Pale blue was a popular color as well as pink for satin ribbon trim and linings.

The long sleeves still have two seams—one in front and one in back. The buttons are not on a normal seam but are on a special opening somewhere in between the two seams.

A soft fabric such as this can have enormous fullness gathered in. This bodice may be constructed in much the same way as the little drawstring dress of Figure 182.

A soft, sheer kerchief is tucked into the neckline in a fashionable, youthful, open style. Much can be said about a woman's age and personality by the way the kerchief is worn (see Figures 166 and 167).

Her large straw hat is put on over the cap of earlier times. It is decorated with satin ribbons. Notice the way the ribbon ties come from the brim. As the brim is pulled down more and more in the next few years, it will develop into the bonnet.

Ringlets around the face were beginning to be worn by fashionable women, again predicting things to come, and the hair is worn long and softly curled.

Figure 170

Figure 171

The new fullness of the bodice shown in Figures 169 and 170 has developed into a full high-waisted dress. These early Empire dresses had drawstrings underneath the bosom and were quite full. Fullness was even added at the shoulder by tucking. Some fastened in back but some overlapped in front for a double-breasted closing.

The woman on the right wears a kerchief tucked loosely into the neckline. Blue-and-white striped or gold-colored taffetas were popular as well as white muslin.

The bonnet (right) is made of a crisp white fabric that looks much like eyelet embroidery. The bonnet has developed a curved band between the crown and the ruffle.

The dress of the woman on the left is of white muslin with a front which crosses over and fastens with a hook and eye. It is edged with braid and a lace ruffle around the neck. The two-part, elbow-length sleeves are divided part-way between the elbow and shoulder by a ruffle; the upper part is made of a lacy embroidered cloth and the lower part matches the dress. This style can also be a dressing gown.

This lady wears a chemise which adds another ruffle to the neckline. The dress is belted with a dark narrow belt with a jeweled buckle.

Her hair is creped and curled with a hot curling iron but only lightly powdered. It, too, reflects the Empire style with the ribbon or gauze wrapped around it. Turbans were becoming popular too.

A little girl's dress is much like her mother's. The bodice has the wide, low neck and fitted sleeves of the period. The neck and sleeves are edged with narrow lace. Her sash is quite wide and tucked or folded to become narrower. The skirt has rows of tucks around the hem. She wears her hair in a shoulder-length, wavy pageboy with straight bangs.

Children's clothes were becoming less restrictive and more comfortable. Since the clothing of sailors and farmers was designed for comfort (and because sailors were popular heroes), little boys' clothing naturally followed their lines.

This little boy wears red sailors' pantaloons.

His red coat is rounded at the corners to become a cutaway. He wears a plain vest over a blouse. His kerchief, worn like that of a woman, is tucked into the neck of the blouse and vest. His hair is a short pageboy with bangs.

Figure 172

Figure 173

1800s

Many Irish artisans and farmers were emigrating to the United States. In 1800 Spain transferred Louisiana Territory to France and in 1803 the United States purchased it from France. As a result many Spanish and French people were automatically made American citizens.

Frontier paths across the mountains were becoming roads—primitive, yes—but roads! Lewis and Clark excited everyone with their report of the Indians and the Western lands. And on both sides of the mountains Yankee pedlars roamed the country practicing free enterprise while supplying necessities and tempting luxuries. Painters or limners were traveling about painting portraits, furniture, walls, or utensils. They were putting likenesses on canvas that would someday tell people in another century what was being worn at the time.

The clothing worn by this man is shown in portraits of presidents, Yankee pedlars, Quakers, young gentlemen, and old men. It is the new cutaway coat, flared top hat, short striped vest, and over-the-chin cravat with the old knee breeches and stockings.

The new coats sometimes had the fold-back lapels of Figure 146. The collar stands high and the cuffs are turned down so that they come down over part of the hands. Coats still fit snugly in the sleeves, shoulders, and chest, but would become fuller in a few years.

Vests were often striped, either vertically or horizontally. The cravat was wrapped around the neck twice and pulled up so high that it came onto the chin. The ends were tied once and tucked into the vest.

This man's hair is cut short in what was called a Brutus cut and brushed toward the face. The new top hats had wide brims and the tops were flared and somewhat soft rather than stiff like later ones.

Early American Costume

(Worn through the 20s.) Even hunting coats had a cutaway appearance as they took on a narrow look. This man wears a fur-trimmed deerskin coat with no collar. It comes to a few inches above the knees.

He wears a white shirt with the collar open and a blue vest which is unbuttoned halfway down the front.

His trousers are particularly interesting as they have one of the earliest side flaps seen down the outside seam. The Indian tribes that migrated from the northern and eastern forests to the plains developed trouser flaps but they were not known to have worn them in the forest where they would catch onto twigs and thorns and be a hindrance. It was the Dakota Indians in particular who developed the wide side flaps after they became plains Indians and began to tame and use horses at the beginning of the 18th century. White men later wore these flaps which by mid-19th century became the cowboy chaps.

He wears boots and a shoulder strap and pouch. His hair is long and parted in the middle and his hat is flat and wide-brimmed.

John James Audubon, the famous botanist, wore a similar coat of wolfskin trimmed with wolf fur. The coat may be seen in his portrait which now hangs in the White House.

Many men were establishing settlements in Kentucky and Tennessee and guiding new groups into the frontier areas. Kentucky had more than 75,000 inhabitants by the end of the 1790s.

Figure 174

The United States navy tired of the piracy of American ships on the Barbary coast of North Africa and decided to fight back! They bombarded the shores of Tripoli while the American marines attacked from the land. Our navy uniforms were developing and would be used in a few years in the War of 1812 (see Figures 188, 189 and 190) but for the time being the navy, marines, and army would all wear much the same clothes.

Our American Army troops at the ceremonies in New Orleans celebrating the Louisiana Purchase in 1803 dressed much like the French Army. Their cutaway uniform coats were curved back so much that the coattails could hardly be seen from the front. The lapels were purely decorative since they could no longer actually be buttoned double-breasted. Their high, stiff, standing collar sometimes was decorated with braid. The coats fasten with two concealed hooks in front over the chest. Officers wear epaulettes (right).

The soldier or marine on the left wears a dark blue coat with lapels of the same dark blue. His vest and breeches are buff. The coattail linings are white as are the straps which cross over his chest. His hat is much like the top hats worn by fashionable men with its rather wide brim and flared top but it appears stiffer, more military. It has a red feather. His boots are black with their buff canvas tops turned down.

The soldier on the right, an officer, wears a dark blue coat with red lapels, collar, and cuffs. The coattail linings are white as is his vest. Over the red breeches he wears leather overalls to protect them. They button all the way down the sides and fasten like breeches in front. These overalls met the Dakota Indian breeches with side flaps a few years later and together they became the cowboy chaps. They were for work duty and riding a horse, not for formal wear.

His hat is a drooping bicorne in the French style. His hair is cut short and brushed toward his face.

Figure 175

A very fashionable lady wears a dress that still has a natural waistline but has the new puff sleeves. Under the drooping puff sleeves are detachable taffeta sleeves which are worn like gloves or mitts (see Figure 169).

Over the dress she wears a kerchief which has a large starched, standing ruffle. The kerchief is worn wide out on the shoulder, then crosses the bosom, and goes around to the back to fasten. A wide sash is tied in back, too, with the long ends hanging down.

Her hair is frizzed out into a round shape and then falls into soft curls around the neck. Her large hat is decorated with plumes.

Figure 176

This high-waisted dress is similar to Figure 171 but there is no fullness to the bodice. It is no longer gathered by a drawstring. This new bodice is fitted, then sewn to a full skirt.

The dress on the left has long tight sleeves which point at the hands. It is beige taffeta with white lace around the neck. The lady wears a white kerchief inside the neck giving a similar appearance to the ruffle-edged kerchief of Figure 155 which is worn outside. It is sometimes difficult to tell one from the other.

Her hair is parted in the middle with bangs and little curls on the cheeks. It is pulled back so that the soft curls form a bun at the neck. She wears drop earrings.

On the right is the same dress with a very different look. This lady wears two kerchiefs (see Figure 155). The first one is a plain white one overlapped in front and held together with a sprig of flowers. Over this she wears another, lace-edged kerchief which is a square folded into a triangle. It is folded so that it forms a lapel or collar making two rows of lace across her bosom and shoulders. It is tied with a ribbon bow.

Her hair is cut short in front and on the sides and combed toward the face while the back hangs free. Her hat is cocked toward the front and decorated with a band and jeweled buckle with one large plume.

Figure 177

121

Early American Costume

After the invention of the cotton gin at the end of the 18th century cotton production was revolutionized in the United States. By this time there were nearly two hundred cotton mills, mostly in New England.

The popularity of French styles and the abundance of cotton cloth together resulted in many soft dresses like this one.

The art works found in the newly excavated ruins of ancient Rome and Greece inspired designs like this dress. It is much like the old Greek chiton with its soft shirred sleeves and bosom. The waistline is up close under the breasts and the skirt is full although it hangs straight because of the softness of the fabric.

The low neckline is filled in with a white embroidered cloth and a neck ruff, called a "betsy" because it was a revival of the old Elizabethan ruff. These neck cloths are not kerchiefs because there are no folds in them. They probably are more like the dickey of the 20th century as is the drawstring blouse worn by the little boy of Figure 212. Some of these dresses had a ruffle all the way around the neckline and some had long sleeves although the length shown seems to have been preferred.

The lady's hair is done in a classic Grecian style with oiled curls and ribbons. Wigs were very common at this time too. She holds a folding fan..

Figure 178

Figure 179

Dresses were made of a soft sheer muslin, gauze, or silk at this time, the more delicate the better. This soft formal gown has a very high Empire waistline and dainty puffed sleeves. The neck is low and wide.

Skirts are straight in front now with the fullness starting at the sides and increasing in the back. This skirt goes into a train at the hem.

Trains varied in length from just a few inches for daytime to several feet long for formal occasions. This dress, like Figure 191, sometimes had a detachable train attached either at the Empire waist or at the shoulders.

A wide satin ribbon crosses the bosom twice, is secured at the shoulders, and tied at the side. The yellow ribbon is embroidered in classic designs of black with a black edge and fringe.

Mitts and gloves which were sometimes as long as sleeves were extremely popular (see Figure 169). They are now worn in bright colors such as orange.

Her Grecian hair style is a wig with little ringlets around her face. She wears black drop earrings.

122

1800-1810

A young lady wears the fashionable style of a few years before as seen in Figures 166, 167, and 168. Overlapping of styles in America occurred for several reasons. Dresses were handed down from mother to daughter as new styles came along. Dresses were bequeathed to family and friends when a woman died. Also, some people in New England and towns on the frontier wore styles of a few years earlier because of their beliefs or because transportation uncertainties made it difficult to acquire the latest fashions.

Her bodice has the neckline which comes below the bosom. It is edged with black braid as are the points of the long, fitted sleeves.

Her chemise shows in front beneath the ruffle-edged kerchief which stands up crisply around her shoulders.

The waistline is raised slightly above the natural waistline and has a dark belt with a jeweled buckle. The full skirt is probably taffeta like the bodice.

She wears a bonnet with old-fashioned lappets hanging from it (see Figure 76).

Her hair is dressed in long soft curls with bangs.

Figure 180

A young girl wears a taffeta dress with a low neck and slightly full sleeves. The bodice is gathered over the bosom as adult dresses were (Figures 169 and 170). Her chemise is pulled up to fill in the neckline with its ruffle standing up. The sleeves of the chemise are turned back over her dress sleeves.

Her skirt is ankle-length and the waist is belted with a wide satin sash, tied in front. Her long hair is parted to the side and hangs in soft curls with a little fringe of bangs on her forehead.

Figure 181

123

Figure 182

A little girl wears a simple muslin dress which has drawstrings at the neck, midriff, and at the waist; they tie in the back. The sleeves are straight, the skirt a few inches off the floor.

Her hair is cut in the Titus style, very short with the ends brushed toward the face.

Her shoes are red, the fashionable color for little girls.

This dress can be made with lace trim and a wide satin sash for a dress-up version. She can wear an apron with it also.

Little boys wore suits with frilly blouses like the one on the left. It is double-breasted with wide lapels and a small collar in a light color. The long trousers are extremely fashionable for this period.

This white blouse has a wide collar with ruffles which continue down into the coat; the cuffs show below the coat sleeves.

He has large buckles on his shoes but little or no tongue flap. His short hair has straight bangs.

The boy on the right, probably a little younger, wears pantaloons and jacket buttoned together for a one-piece-suit effect. The ankle-length, full pantaloons have a flap construction like adult breeches. They button onto the jacket all the way around.

His blouse has a wide ruffled collar extending to the shoulder line. It might be a sleeveless, drawstring blouse like that of Figure 212.

He wears white stockings and low-cut slippers. His hair is worn in a long pageboy with bangs.

Figure 183

124

1810s

The great wave of immigrants, which would total five million by the middle of the century, was in full swing. Immigrants poured in to the United States from many countries, but mostly from Ireland, England, and Germany.

The stage coach, Conestoga wagon, and the steamboat made it easier for them to get to the western areas across the Appalachians even though travel was still rough.

Some men in the frontier areas wore much the same fashionable clothing as men back east—probably the leading citizens of the settlements.

This gentleman's cutaway tailcoat was very fashionable. These coats were both double-breasted and single-breasted, according to preference. The high collar sometimes went up to the ears, with boning in it to keep it from drooping. Shoulders were wide, with the armhole down onto the arm just a bit. The sleeves were gathered in at the shoulder, full at the upper arm, and close-fitting from the elbow, the cuffs worn down over the hands. This makes them curve in at the wrist and then flare out as they are split. For a rear view, see the shorter version in Figure 185.

The shirt has a front frill and the cravat goes around twice, then ties in a knot at the neck. The shirt sleeve ruffle shows at the hand.

Lapels are also on the vest, which is longer than the shortened coat front. Watches and watch fobs without a watch were so popular that two of them were often worn at once.

Breeches and pantaloons were many lengths at this time. Breeches were much longer than in previous years, coming down onto the calf. They buttoned high up the leg onto the thigh, sometimes even all the way to the waist. The new breeches were high-waisted so as to go up under the new vests and short coats. Ties at the calf were the latest thing, sometimes hanging down several inches. The breeches have the front flap construction and were often made of natural leather.

This man wears natural leather gaiters which button up the side with a little tab at the top for buttoning onto one of the breeches buttons. His shoes are low-heeled black slippers. The new hats are tall flared top hats with wider brims than they would have at the end of the decade.

His hair is the new Brutus cut introduced by the French who had been inspired by the ancient Greek and Roman hair styles. It is cut short, oiled, and brushed toward the face with sideburns down on the cheeks.

For overcoats of the period, see Figure 199.

Figure 184

Figure 185

(Worn through the 30s.) Coats as well as breeches varied in length for several years before they both became longer. They varied from the long calf or even ankle-length coats which were already being worn to very short jackets like those of Figure 189. Any of the coats from 1800 through 1830 can be worn during this period because of the overlapping of styles.

These young men wear the short tails probably favored by younger and more adventurous men. From the front they look as if the tails are cut off. From the rear the coat looks surprisingly 20th century. The collar stands up in back but falls down in front with rounded corners on both collar and lapels. The collar and lapels are sewn together part of the way instead of being entirely separate as in Figure 184.

One 1812 eyewitness watercolor painted in an inn on the way west by Russian artist Paul Svinin shows people dancing to the music of a fiddle. They are shown from several views, full length. One man wears a suit of small brown plaid or check. His sleeves have the cuffs turned up like that shown. The rear view shows the back seams and the pocket flaps which are almost invisible from the front. It also shows the back split which is still trimmed with braid as tails have been for more than one hundred years (see Figure 92). When buttoned, this coat is quite tight in the waist as is Figure 184. (This painting hangs in the Metropolitan Museum of Art.)

Vests were often horizontally striped with satin backs.

The shirt collar is open and stands up against his cheeks with the cravat wrapped around it and tied in a small knot in front. Red cravats were appearing at this time in most areas of America.

The man on the left wears striped pantaloons which come to the ankles and are quite form-fitting. They have a little split at the ankle. In one diary of the period a gentleman told how, when he removed his skintight corduroy pantaloons, his legs had fluted impressions of the cloth left on them!

This man wears the popular watch fob and flat, pointed slippers with bows. The hat in the front view is a flared narrow-brimmed top hat which has become stiff. The brim is curled up on the sides and down in front and back. The rear view shows the other style with a crown which is smaller toward the top. Some are even smaller at the crown, being almost conical. The hair is curly with long sideburns.

The black fiddle player in the painting mentioned above wears an almost identical outfit of brown pantaloons, green coat, and black conical hat (on rear view). His cuffs were turned up also. His coattails were ragged on the edge as though they really had been cut off! And the men, and women too (Figure 192), have red bandanas around their necks—long before western cowboys started wearing them.

126

1810-1820

In the Battle of New Orleans General Andrew Jackson had an army made up of regular troops, Choctaw Indians, pirates, and backwoodsmen from Tennessee. Obviously there was an assortment of clothing.

Some of the uniforms were much like those of Figure 175 (left) but were bright blue instead of dark blue. Jackson, and William Henry Harrison in his defeat of the British and Indians at the Battle of Thames in Canada, wore uniforms like this officer.

His dark blue coat has tails so small that they barely cover the buttocks. From the front it looks as though there are no tails. The stand-up collar goes to just under the ears. It is cut at an angle so that it slants back instead of poking the chin. The body and sleeves are very form-fitting. Most of these coats were single-breasted although a few portraits of the period show them double-breasted. This one has braid trim the same color as the coat and brass buttons. It has two (sometimes three) rows of braid on the collar and cuffs and gold epaulettes.

His white pantaloons are form-fitting. The riding boots are cut lower in back than in front so as to fit the curve of the leg when it is bent. The flap closings on the breeches now have fly bindings on them.

He wears white gloves with flared gauntlets and a plumed bicorne with the corners front and back instead of side to side. He wears a yellow officer's sash around his waist and a cravat at his neck.

A regulation of 1812 prescribed red cuffs and collars with white braid trim for enlisted men in the infantry. They also wore the long trousers with the strap under the foot shown in Figure 148.

Figure 186

Westward-bound settlers were guided through the mountains by frontiersmen who would rather sleep under the stars than under a roof. These "over mountain men" were followed by fur traders, southern stockmen (our earliest cowboy), hunters, and farmers until by the first decade of the 19th century more than 300,000 people had migrated through the Cumberland Gap.

The earliest settlers lived in caves, hunted for their food, and lived much like the Indians. Some accounts tell of women wearing Indian deerskin dresses and moccasins after their clothes wore out but there are no known eyewitness sketches to show them.

The frontiersman's coat is snug-fitting like fashionable coats with the stylish stand-up collar and long sleeves with fullness at the shoulder. It has a cape around the shoulders for double protection against rain. It is trimmed with narrow fringe. He wears a wide leather belt and a strap over his shoulder holding a pouch and canteen. He wears a white shirt underneath with the neck open.

His breeches are tight-fitting with a fringe down the side seams. Indian moccasins are the favored footwear. His hat is the conical top hat of a gentleman (like that of Figure 185). These tall hats were commonly worn with hunting clothes in wilderness areas.

Coats were trimmed with fur in winter, possibly because the fur was inside. They were made of blue dyed canvas or linen for the summer months. Chester Harding's engraving of Daniel Boone shows him in a coat like this with the top hat. Explorer James Pattie, in his published account, *Unheard of Hardships and Dangers* (1831), pictured himself wearing the top hat while on a raft on a wilderness river! He also wore the long hunting coat with shoulder cape.

Figure 187

Early American Costume

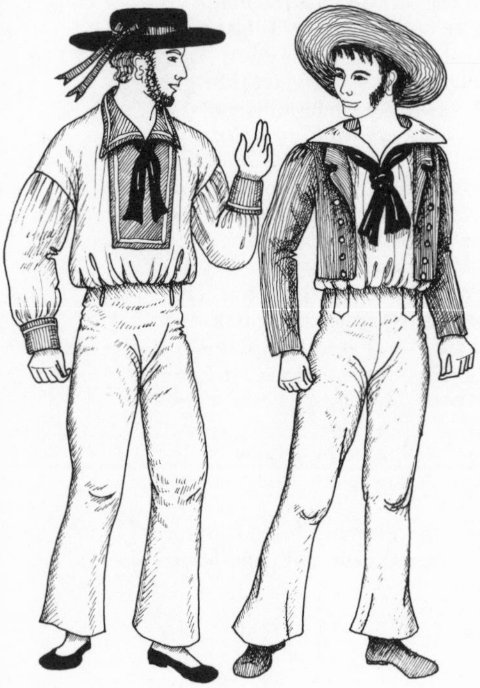

Naval battles during the War of 1812 were fought in top hats, stocking caps, plaid shirts, vests, and dress coats, in other words whatever the men happened to have on, but there were some uniforms for both officers and seamen.

This seaman's uniform (left) has a white shirt much like regular shirts with its drop shoulders and full body. It has blue cuffs, collar, and front bib or panel trimmed with white braid. He wears a black kerchief tied under the collar. This is probably just the black cravat. His full white pantaloons come to the ankles above his flat, low-cut black slippers.

His hat is the wide-brimmed one worn by farmers for many years. The crown is flattened to become the sailor hat with streamers from the band. Sailors and farmers have had similar forms of dress for centuries, probably because their work exposes them to the elements and because they are both known to be independent sorts who insist on functional, comfortable clothes. His hair is curly with the sideburns extending into a small beard.

On the right a sailor wears a short jacket. These short jackets appeared on men and boys on Mississippi River barges as well as in seaport towns. Shipbuilders and dock workers as well as sailors and canal workers wore the open collar with a tie, often red, and the short jacket. Young boys and very small boys have worn the sailor suit even into the 20th century.

These jackets were very short, about to the waist in most cases, but sometimes a little below or above. They were usually double-breasted with a collar and lapels and long fitted sleeves.

The shirt is much the same as the one on the left but without the blue trim. They still open only part of the way down the front. The cravat is loosely tied under the open collar. The fullness of the shirt blouses out under the jacket a little.

Pantaloons and breeches had a new fly binding on the flap closings now, as shown on the right. The lower leg shows signs of developing a flare or bell which would become even more pronounced in a few more years.

His shoes are high-topped ones which disappear under the pantaloons. The hat is the wide-brimmed, low-crowned hat which would eventually be called a "sailor." English sailors wore this same jacket, shirt, and tie with the traditional petticoat breeches of Figures 61 and 127. These were long worn by European sailors and called "slops."

Figure 188

The Revolutionaries of Paris during the French Revolution adopted the coat of the working class as a symbol. The short jacket has through the centuries been associated with sailors, farmers, peasants, laborers, and young protestors so it was chosen to be theirs. It was soon refined to a fashionable coat but remained identified with men of the sea who wore it first and with young daring men and little boys.

One New England businessman wore it; his business was making nautical instruments. He, like this man, wore the top hat and a red vest which comes up even higher on the cheeks than the coat collar. The shirt collar and cravat are like those of Figure 185 only the cravat is black.

The breeches are the full pantaloons or loose trousers which stop at the ankle. His slippers are very low and black with little bows.

This dark coat is virtually the same as that of Figure 184 without the tails. The cuffs turn down onto the hands also.

It simply is not possible to tell in a great many portraits if this coat has tails or not so there is no way to know how extensively it was worn by gentlemen. An 1815 painting by German artist John Lewis Krimmel shows a man in Philadelphia wearing such a coat but he is a working man carrying a sign.

Originally the cravat was used symbolically during the French Revolution. Red meant "off with their heads" and black meant mourning for the beheaded aristocrats. This might also explain the red cravat often seen in America where it was worn like the sailor ties of Figure 188 or sometimes tied in a bow. Either these young men, and they are always young, are French immigrants, just young men who like to wear something associated with protest, or they are sailors.

Some of the men aboard the American ship *Chesapeake* in 1813 engaged in battle wearing this short coat, pantaloons, and top hats! One wore a red vest like this man and another a red stocking cap.

Figure 189

1810-1820

American naval officers of the War of 1812 wore dark blue coats with the tails lined with white. Most were double-breasted, usually buttoned, but occasionally worn with the lapels buttoned back. The high stand-up collar came up onto the cheeks with a stand-up shirt collar and black cravat underneath. High officers had gold braid on the collar, lapels, and cuffs, with gold epaulettes and swords.

Most admirals left the top three or four buttons unbuttoned and the lapels turned back showing much gold braid on the inside.

Being a naval officer, this man wears the traditional white pantaloons, usually pictured quite loose. His black hat is a bicorne with gold braid and pompon, which has grown quite large and drooping. He wears it with the corners front and back.

Figure 190

Although some of the newer dresses were losing their front fullness, many still had some gathers in front. The drawstring was not used anymore. The skirt and bodice were gathered and pleated separately before being sewn together. Instead of gathers in back there was more likely to be a number of pleats folded in so that the skirt was quite full. Most formal dresses went into trains in back—the more formal the occasion, the longer the train. Sometimes the long trains were like long aprons on the back and were detachable.

The neckline of this lady's dress is quite low and wide. The sleeves are full and gathered onto a band but they do not puff up at the shoulders. They are flared in shape so that most of the fullness is at the lower part. The fabrics are soft and thin and the fullness falls almost in a straight line.

She wears the *extra* sleeves which are attached up under the dress sleeve as described in Figure 169. While the dresses are mostly white or pale colors these sleeves or mitts are bright colors such as orange, yellow, bright pink, green, or blue.

Embroidery is a popular trim, either crewel worked in bright colors, or all one color and sometimes gold or silver on formal dresses. Some embroidery done with straw imitated gold embroidery so successfully that it was difficult to believe it was not gold!

She wears her hair in a Grecian design with ringlets around her face. The ankle-length pantalets worn underneath are like those worn by the little girls of Figures 211 and 223. At first the pantalets were not really pants but just leggings, like those of Indians, from the knee down.

Figure 191

129

Early American Costume

This dress was seen on pioneers traveling into the backwoods, young ladies out strolling, and on Presidents' wives like Dolly Madison and Elizabeth Monroe. It was worn by all kinds and all ages of women. It is shown here in just two of its many variations.

On the left a young woman wears the gathered bodice which is sewn to a very plain skirt front. In back the skirt is full and the bodice fitted. The sleeves are less full than those of Figure 191 as is the skirt front. There is a little binding around the neckline and she wears a sash tied in front. The skirt is a few inches off the floor.

The kerchief around her neck is worn by almost all women at this time. Prints are immensely popular, especially with red backgrounds. Along with the kerchief she wears a long narrow stole shown draped in the typical manner, over one arm and under the other (see Figure 197 also).

Long gloves with scalloped tops and a cylindrical bonnet complete her outfit. A ribbon goes over the top of the bonnet and ties under the chin. The little girl of Figure 224 holds a similar one of straw. It fits over the hair styles of Figures 179 and 191.

The woman on the right wears the same dress in silk print fabric with a border around the hem. Her cape has two tiers and two collars. One collar lies down flat while the other stands up. It is fastened with two buttons and a loop. These capes had fur on the edges for cold weather. Such lightweight, small capes and stoles were often all that was added for warmth even in severe New England winters.

Turbans (like that on the right) were often wrapped with two different fabrics or gauze and decorated with a plume. Her hair has little oiled ringlets around the face.

She wears long gloves and drop earrings. Pantalets are worn underneath the dress.

Figure 192

It seemed as if the whole world was buying American cotton! By 1800 we were exporting five million dollars worth and by 1810 it was fifteen million. Immigrants were coming to America by the thousands from Ireland, England, and Germany. Many of them were traveling west but others stayed in the East to work in cotton mills which numbered in the hundreds by this time. These mills provided the first out-of-the-home employment for young women. Many songs and stories were written about the life of the mill girl.

A young woman (right) wears the universally popular high-waisted dress like that of Figure 192 with a ruffle at the hem. Here are front and back views of the apron worn in the mills. Made of muslin or linen, it has a wide neck and large armholes leaving a very narrow shoulder strap. It is straight with ties in the back. The top ties are short while the ones a few inches lower are quite long. These long ties cross in back and tie in front, so that the apron appears to have a waistline like the dress. Sometimes the aprons were worn straight. This is much like the apron worn by women at home and by slaves and servants also. It sometimes was white, natural unbleached, gray, or gray-blue. Some aprons had pockets, some did not.

The rear view (left) shows the cloth bonnet with the starched, sometimes quilted, brim which became so identified with 19th century America. The woman on the right wears a little turban bonnet much like the bonnets of earlier years but without the ruffle around the face. It has a sewn-in crown and ribbon decorations. Her oiled ringlets hang out around her face and neck.

She wears the new pointed laced shoes which come up higher on the foot than the little slippers.

Many young women of all walks of life were wearing red bandanas on their heads, tied either under the chin or on top of the head like a turban.

Figure 193

130

1810-1820

The high waistline shows some sign of beginning to move back down on this very new dress at the end of the decade. It also predicts the large sleeves to come. It was worn by very fashionable women and made in checks, small plaids, and calicos.

This one has a fitted bodice which has darts under the breasts instead of gathers. It is tucked between the breasts to make it form-fitting and at the same time pulls the neckline down into a dip. This neckline is wide but somewhat higher than in recent years.

The sleeves were gathered at the shoulder but only at the top. They were large at the upper arm and tapered until they became more fitted below the elbow. They did not puff up, but fell or drooped from the shoulder giving a sloping shoulder look. These sleeves were long enough to cover the hands completely; they wrinkled on the arm and flared out over the hand. Many sleeves had a little belt-like band of matching fabric around the wrist with a button to hold the sleeve in its proper position.

All the skirt fullness was at the sides and back; the front was slightly flared, letting the fabric flow softly down over the body.

Decorations around the skirt hems were elaborate and bulky. All kinds of puffs, twists, swags, ruffles, and braids were used, giving the skirts a stiff look. Skirt lengths were raised off the floor, revealing the flat-heeled shoes.

This woman wears the coal-scuttle or basket bonnet. It has a high, flared crown and a wide brim, wider in front than in back. The ribbons come from the crown, sometimes across it, and over the brim, holding it in close to the face. This bonnet was usually straw as straw hats were first manufactured in America at the end of the 18th century.

She holds a purse decorated with beads and tassels. The form-fitting skirts made the old pockets of Figure 107 go out of style and the purse became a necessity.

Figure 194

Figure 195

The Empire coat called a redingote remained fashionable for a number of years. They appeared in several lengths from the floor up to the knees. Some were worn knee-length in order to show the elaborate skirt decorations on the dresses. These coats, although more sensible than the small capes and stoles, did not replace them. The stole and shawl continued to be enough for many women into the 1850s.

This woman wears a velvet coat trimmed with fur. The bodice is fitted and the skirt flared in front and gathered or pleated quite full in back. The sleeves are like those of the dress in Figure 194.

Double fasteners were used such as two buttons with a hook closing as shown or sometimes two frogs. Ties were also used and even little straps attached to each side with buckles like a belt.

The cape comes to the high waistline and has a stand-up flared collar.

Her bonnet is like that of Figure 194 but is made of velvet and trimmed with fur to match the coat and muff.

Trims other than fur were large braids or bands of satin or velvet on wool coats. Various puffs and swags like those on the dresses were used too.

131

Early American Costume

Formal gowns were quite complex in their decoration at this time. This gown bodice is much like that of Figure 192 with small puffed sleeves and a gathered bosom. The skirt is flared in front and pleated full in the back and sides like that of Figure 194 only with more flare.

This lady wears a gown of a pastel-colored sheer fabric. It is worn over a lining of satin of the same color. The satin is used for ruffles which have been cut in scallops with a pinking tool, making still smaller scallops on the edges. These pinked, scalloped ruffles are used on the neck, sleeves, and skirt. The flowers and leaf designs, also of satin, are appliquéd on. This satin on sheer over satin technique gives an interesting feeling of depth. Done in white, cream, or gray, this was used for wedding dresses.

Her hair is pulled up in a topknot of curls around her face and neck. They are more curls than ringlets now.

She wears beads around her neck and long formal gloves. She holds a folding fan.

Figure 196

Figure 197

Women were now seeking equal educational opportunity, and girls' seminaries were opening in cities and towns all over America. At first they were directed toward manners and homemaking arts—the so-called "finishing schools"—but at least girls were receiving some sort of an education.

This very fragile young lady wears a soft sheer white high-waisted Empire dress. The neck is low and the dainty sleeves are so small that they end above where the neck begins. The sleeves and neckline have a small binding around the edge. There are gathers above and below the bosom, but the sleeves are gathered only at the arm and not at the shoulder. Sometimes there were buttons on each shoulder to hold a kerchief or a stole in place. The fabric of these dresses was like lawn or batiste. This one has several rows of ruffles around the hem with a row of pink flowers and green leaves, although skirts were often plain, too.

She wears her green stole in the fashionable way. Girls often went out in winter, even snow, in one of these thin dresses with only a tiny cloth stole like this for warmth. She wears pantalets underneath.

Her hair is interesting in the way it is parted. First it is parted on her left, then the section in front of her ear on the left side is pulled forward and across her forehead where it is held in place with a comb and ends in little ringlets. The rest of the hair on her left is pulled to the back to join the locks from the top and right side which are pulled back. All this long hair is then twisted and pulled up the back of the head and held with a large decorative comb.

She wears drop earrings, rings, and a necklace with two strands of beads holding a brooch. She carries a drawstring purse. Her tan slippers are open on top and have little tabs with ties.

132

Figure 198

The highwaisted styles are particularly charming on little girls. This little girl's dress is much like those of adults except that the bodice needs no fullness. The skirt is plain in front and full in back. It is a green wool dress with dark pink buttonhole-stitched scallops around the hem. Her narrow sash is the same pink.

Her hair is braided, then wrapped around her head. Pink ribbons are worn on top. She wears high-topped red shoes and long pantalets. Her sun bonnet, like that of Figure 193, lies on the floor beside her.

Little boys' clothes which often imitate their mothers' have high waists too. The blouse has a wide collar edged with lace and long sleeves which come down onto the hands like adult clothes.

His very high-waisted pantaloons button onto the blouse and are split at the ankles. His shoes are high-topped button shoes.

His hair is worn long and parted in the middle.

CHAPTER 7

Old Traditions Mix with New

1820 to 1850

Figure 199

1820s

The Erie Canal was completed in 1825 and stage coaches were making regular runs between cities. River travel was bustling with keelboats and flatboats with a few new steamboats appearing on the Ohio, Mississippi, and Missouri Rivers. The textile mills became a major American industry. Gold was discovered in Georgia and Tennessee.

Norwegian farmers, laborers, cotters, and servants were emigrating to the United States in great numbers, many of them joining the settlers moving westward.

(Worn through the 40s) The new long breeches brought about two new ideas in men's clothing: suspenders and short stockings. The double frill at the neckline was no longer fashionable. When a frill was worn it was only a single one on just one side of the shirt opening.

Men's cloaks of the first half of the 19th century included both capes and long overcoats.

The Polish-style cape had one, sometimes two, or three short capes around the shoulders. The large collar stood up around the neck where the cape was fastened, usually with just one fastener.

Both coats and capes varied from floor to finger-tip length, depending on the length of the jacket or suit coat underneath.

Coats like that on the right have tight waists and full skirts. The sleeves are full at the upper arm where they are gathered a little at the shoulder. They taper to become fitted from the elbow down with the cuffs worn down over the hands. Notched collars like those of Figure 200 are worn on these coats as well as the shawl collar shown here. This one is fur. Buttons go only to the waistline and the coat skirt is open. Pantaloons, trousers with straps, or knee breeches are worn underneath. Coats like the capes were seen in almost any length although the long ones were favored.

The top hat was the fashion as the tricorne and bicorne were no longer worn by gentlemen.

Figure 200

Coats now had rounded lapels with shallow notches and sometimes no notches at all. Although they were usually double-breasted, they were most often worn unbuttoned. They fitted very snugly in the waist and chest while the upper sleeves still had some fullness, although less than a few years ago. The armholes were smaller now but with shoulder padding. Sleeves were still long but not down to the knuckles. Buttons were set so they came closer at the waist, giving a "V" appearance.

The tails began about halfway between center front and the side seam. Rounded so that they cupped in around the hips, they were longer than in recent years, coming to or even below the knees. Tails still had braid trim down the back split. Brown, green, and gray were favorite colors.

Vests were single-breasted with the buttons stopping at the chest and the lapels rounded.

The new shirts had tucked fronts and sometimes no frill at all. The cravat was wrapped around the neck and tied in front in a small knot but no longer went up over the chin. White satin cravats were worn for formal occasions.

Trousers still had double openings but were pleated or tucked at the waist so that they rounded out over the hips, then tapered to the ankles. They buttoned at the ankles, up to the knees or sometimes all the way up the sides like military overalls (see Figure 175). They varied from knee-length for old men, to calf, ankle, and full length with a strap under the foot. Trousers were going through an experimental stage before settling on the long ones which would remain fashionable for 150 years. Favorite fabrics for trousers were stockinet and doeskin in light colors such as gray, beige, yellow, with cream and white for summer. Watch fobs were still worn.

Patent leather was invented in America in 1822 so this gentleman wears patent leather boots with pointed toes. After Mr. Macintosh in England invented waterproof cloth, by 1830 men were wearing raincoats and capes like the overcoat of Figure 199. One popular style of coat is like that in Figure 199 with the shoulder capes like those on the Polish cloak.

The top hat of both conical and straight designs was worn. Men parted their hair and brushed it down on each side into sideburns. The top was brushed forward but instead of being flat as before, it was puffed up, rather high sometimes.

Both pipe smoking and snuff dipping were popular. Pipes had been used for a long time but a new invention, the wooden match, made it more convenient. The first match invented in 1805 had to be ignited by dipping it into a bottle of sulphuric acid!

137

Early American Costume

Immigrants continued to pour into New York. The men arrived wearing clothes like these—the clothes of farmers, miners, lumbermen, riverboat men. (See Figure 202.)

Working men everywhere took up the newly invented suspenders. (Belt loops and leather belts were not worn until the 20th century.)

Shirts were still full-bodied with full sleeves and drop shoulders. The shirt opened only part of the way down the front. Working men wore the collar either buttoned or open, sometimes with bandanas. Colored shirts were worn, too, especially red or blue.

Trousers and pantaloons were high-waisted and sometimes quite loose. They were made from a variety of fabrics from homespun to canvas to leather.

This man wears the English riding boots favored by lumbermen, miners, and farmers. They have canvas-lined tops turned down with the boot straps showing. Some have red linings instead of buff.

The large round hat is worn plain but many men pushed the crown into various shapes, at the same time rolling the brim in individual ways. This hat was to become the cowboy hat at mid-century.

Figure 201

Figure 202

Denim was worn in the Middle Ages and is said to have originated in France. It has always been associated with functional working clothes and with sailors. It has sometimes been called canvas although denim has indigo blue threads going one way and white the other.

French Revolutionists took up the clothes of working people and sailors. Many sailors, Frenchmen, and other Europeans were coming to America by the thousands at this time. Denim pantaloons were worn by miners too. It was principally these early miners and sailors who popularized denim and took it to the frontier.

Texas cowboys refused to wear denim at first because the ranch hands wore it, but they eventually discovered its advantages. Cattlemen had been driving herds of cattle in Louisiana, Georgia, and Tennessee since the late 18th century so cowmen had been at work a long time before cattle drives were made in Texas.

The billed cap brought by immigrants from Europe appeared in every part of the country on miners, river men, laborers, lumbermen, musicians, and steel workers. It was very much a part of the American scene as was the red bandana which the man on the left wears on his neck, and the one on the right wears on his head.

The full, drop-shoulder shirts were worn in many ways and several colors. Red was popular as well as blue, green, and black.

Vests were either buttoned or open. Most during this period had satin backs. Pantaloons were tucked into the boots (as in Figure 201), rolled up, or just loose.

Red cravats from France were worn around the open collar as shown by the man on the right. Red stocking caps of ancient origin also were commonly seen among the men moving west. A variety of footwear was seen, too, everything from military boots to slippers with bows to bare feet.

Many of the black men along the Missouri and Mississippi Rivers wore this outfit with large hats or bandanas on their head. Men tied the bandana with the knot to the back or side of the head.

Young boys wore both of these outfits as much as men did.

138

People still went west by flatboat or on foot even though the stage coach was commonly used in the East. Roads through the mountains and in the wilderness territory were rough paths.

When new areas had 5,000 people, they could become an official territory with a legislature and representation. When they got 16,000 inhabitants they could apply for statehood as some territories were doing at this time.

Many men in the backwoods owned and wore fashionable clothes at times but deerskin clothes were still the most practical for those whose work took them into wilderness areas. Men in the eastern states still wore hunting clothes at times too. Linen was the fabric used for summer or mild weather.

This deerskin coat reflects current styles with its shawl collar and cape. The skirt appears to be flared somewhat and it probably has a split in the back as all coats do. It is trimmed with fur around the neck, front, hem, sleeves, and cape.

This hunter wears a black cravat with the points of the collar showing above and a wide leather belt. His pantaloons are deerskin also and fit snugly to the ankles over his moccasins.

The shoulder strap holds a powder horn and pouch. His round hat has fur trim like his coat. Sometimes these hats had a small animal tail attached like that in Figure 113.

A large number of coats of this period had fur trim.

Figure 203

Figure 204

The Empire style was still quite fashionable in America although the waist showed signs of returning to its natural position and sleeves were growing larger in Europe at this time.

This lady has the low neck filled in with a sheer embroidered cloth. It is no longer a kerchief, but probably a dickey that ties under the bosom much like the little boy's blouse of Figure 212. Some were sewn to the dress as a yoke. Around her neck she wears a ruff called a "betsy" (see Figure 178). Some women wore just the ruff on a bare neck. Older ladies liked the ruff too and continued to wear it for some time to hide an aging neck.

The bodice has dainty puffed sleeves and a very high waistline up under the bosom. The neckline is low. The long sleeves at this time were often separate sleeves, even a different fabric (see Figure 169). These have a flounce at the wrist and are the same fabric as the dress.

The skirt is only slightly flared in front with no gathers but full in back. It is a little off the floor, showing the flat slippers.

Her hair has oiled ringlets around her face with curls piled up on the crown. She wears a headband, large loop earrings, and a ring on her index finger.

Early American Costume

Figure 205

A young lady wears a dress remarkable for its amount of decoration. It is pale blue satin or taffeta with an Empire waistline. The bodice is gathered both above and below the breasts. It has little puffed sleeves of the same blue fabric as the dress, then three rows of white shirring which are puffed out to form rolls, then full sleeves of the blue with white shirred cuffs.

The belt is white satin ribbon with an amber beaded brooch. The skirt has two rows of white satin pulled up in swags. The neckline, rather high, is circled with a double ruffle of sheer lace. Half of it lies down on the dress and the other half stands up, indicating that it is crisp rather than soft.

She wears a white lace shawl because lace could be made by machine at this time and was available in large pieces for shawls and veils.

Pantaloons were still often just tied around the leg below the knees. The new soft clinging dresses of the last few years required new, soft, clinging petticoats. The idea of the leggings came about because women needed something to show around the hem of the shorter dresses. But women found long pantalets as strange as men found the long trousers; so for a few years they used leggings instead. By this time the idea of wearing pantaloons, or pantalets, as women's were called, seemed less strange.

Her shoes are pale blue with jeweled brooches and ties around the ankles. Her white satin purse is decorated with amber beads like those on her belt. Her earrings match her bead necklace which circles her neck and then holds her lace collar down in front.

Her hair is sectioned off in front and parted in the middle. Combs hold these sections in bunches of ringlets at the temples and cheeks. The rest of the hair is pulled back, twisted, and held in place with a large fan comb.

Figure 206

The dress shown here is taken from a painting dated 1826 done in Tennessee by Ralph Earl, one of America's early limners. The dress is a few years behind the fashion, indicating a lag in getting over the mountains. But the hair style is the very latest! This is an excellent example of cultural lag due to distance, and shows that the young woman was in close enough contact with the East to know what the new hair styles were. Figure 205 is based on a similar situation in St. Louis.

This soft dress of a deep yellow or gold color has a high Empire waistline with a belt of matching fabric and a jeweled buckle. The neckline is high compared to most. It is filled in with a soft kerchief. All the skirt fullness is in the back. The very long sleeves are loose at the upper arm but form-fitting from the elbow down with cuffs which go partly over the hands. Pointed caps at the shoulders are sewn in with the sleeves; they are made of the same fabric tucked in rows.

The lady's hair is much like that of Figure 205 but instead of small combs holding the curls on each side, she has two very large, curved combs, one crossed over the other forming an "X" on top of her head. The back hair is wrapped around a large comb standing up at the crown.

This simple woolen dress is charming in its simplicity. It has a high waistline but indicates that waistlines are moving down. The high neck has a crisp ruff or "betsy" of several layers. The sleeves are growing fuller and even though they taper in at the elbow they remain somewhat loose to the wrist where they flow out onto the hands and end with a dainty ruffle.

The skirt is fitted in front with only a little flare at the hem, with considerable fullness gathered in at the back. Several rows of cording are sewn in, causing slight puckering as cording does and holding the skirt out around the hem.

The dress is olive green with a pink sash and a white lacy ruff around the neck. The bonnet is white also; it is like the bonnet of Figure 208 which can be viewed from the side. It is made with the fullness at the crown so that it fits over the topknot hair styles of Figures 204, 205, and 206.

Figure 207

Figure 208

Although this dress has an apron, here it does not necessarily mean that the dress is only for working. It is quite similar to Figure 207 but new for the period with its front-buttoned bodice. The dress is made of a soft pinkish gray fabric with a collar of the same fabric. Inside the collar is a crisp white lace standing ruffle. It is actually two layers of lace. The front buttons are pearl. The sleeves are gathered at the shoulder with fullness at the upper arm, tapering to a fitted wrist. The gathers are only at the top of the shoulders; they do not continue down the side of the sleeve at the armhole. The long sleeves go out over the hand almost to the knuckles with a little strap and pearl button around each wrist to hold them in place.

The skirt is fitted with a slight flare in front and gathered or pleated full in back. A narrow belt of the same fabric ties around the high waist.

The apron has a narrow waistband which ties around the Empire waist and slender straps over the shoulder which do not cross in back. The pockets are gathered full with a lace ruffle at the top. Aprons are sometimes black or gray as well as white and unbleached.

The high crown of the bonnet makes room for the topknot of the lady's hair. The band is shaped to fit the head like a cap and points toward the chin. A ruffle goes all the way around and even continues beyond the point, making the ruffle go under the chin to the ties, which are usually satin ribbon.

141

Early American Costume

(Worn through the 30s.) A prediction of the styles of the 30s is seen in this transitional dress. The waistline seam is lower than it has been in several years although it is still above the natural waistline. Sleeves have grown large and puffed out, and the extra sleeve or mitt is worn under the full sleeve. The bodice has an interesting "V" neckline which is filled in with a panel of matching fabric.

The skirt has developed fullness on the sides of the front by this time and is quite full. Dresses are still one to three inches off the floor.

The most beautiful part of this dress and several similar ones is the embroidery which uses the popular wheat and laurel leaf designs. Formal gowns were usually white satin or taffeta with gold embroidery. Muslin dresses with crewel embroidery done in blue and brown or in bright colors like blue-green, pinks, yellow, dull reds, blues, and other bright colors were worn too. These crewel yarns were dyed with vegetable dyes and varied according to locality. Women in the eastern coastal cities could get imported yarns already dyed.

Straw was used as a substitute for the expensive gold thread during the late 18th and early 19th centuries. It looks astonishingly like gold on one pink taffeta dress in the Boston Museum of Fine Arts.

Her hair is worn in a large topknot with the front hair parted and pulled to the sides in ringlets held by small combs. Ribbons and leaves are fastened to the topknot.

Her necklace has bead swags hanging from it. Each swag has a large bead or stone. She holds a folding fan.

Figure 209

Figure 210

A young boy wears a blue-and-white striped vest with a double-breasted, dark green coat and pantaloons. The lapels have an interesting point shape. Even though the very short jacket is double-breasted, it would be quite tight if buttoned. These short jackets were rarely, if ever, buttoned. The pantaloons are full and come to the ankle.

His shirt has a wide collar which is starched so that it stands out from his neck and then folds over. His shoes are black, flat slippers. He wears a red watch fob like adults' and his hair, also like adults', is combed forward.

142

A little girl (left) wears a dress which has changed little from the last decade except that it has more fullness in the skirt and sleeves. This red dress has several rows of black braid around the hem reminiscent of the old rural bands of the 17th century. The neckline and sleeve bands are black also. The high waistline has a drawstring which ties in the back.

Her hair style is new—bunched curls high up over the ears with just a wisp of bangs at the center part. She wears beads around her neck and black slippers.

On the right a little girl wears a calico dress with matching pantalets. The gathered sleeves are full over the upper arms, taper to the wrist, and come out over the hands like those of Figures 207 and 208. This dress even imitates the adult dresses with a gathered bosom on the high-waisted bodice. The wide square neck has a ruffle around it.

The skirt has fullness only at the sides and back and a flounce around the hem. It is rather short—almost calf length—showing the calico pantalets and black shoes.

Her hair is cut short and brushed toward the face in little points.

Figure 211

Figure 212

Little boys wear the short jacket of Figure 189 and will continue to wear it for many years as they will the sailor suit.

The boy on the left wears the suit of a dark fabric, velvet for dress-up, cotton for everyday. The jacket is collarless with small buttons down the front. The full, ankle-length pantaloons have a drop-seat panel in back.

The boy in the middle shows the little drawstring, sleeveless blouse which is worn over the pantaloons and camisole top seen on the boy on the right.

The blouse of the little boy on the left has a ruffle for a collar but is essentially the same as that worn by the boy in the middle. When his outfit is complete he wears black slippers and a top hat like adults.

143

Early American Costume

A very little girl (left) is dressed in white with white eyelet trim, which consists of two different kinds of eyelet, one a straight band with flowers and the other straight on one side with points on the other. The little Empire bodice is edged at the neck with the pointed eyelet which turns down in a cuff. The tiny sleeves are two rows of the same lace joined so that the points are on both sides. They are caught with red bows. The skirt is gathered slightly and comes to her calf. The hem is trimmed with two rows of the straight lace and a row of the points.

Her high-top shoes are bright red, her bonnet is red, black, and green plaid with a white ruffle around the face and white plumes on top. It has a red bow in front. (The plaid design of the bonnet fabric is omitted here so that the lines of the bonnet can be clearly seen.) It has a Scottish feeling to it.

She wears a miniature portrait on a cord around her neck.

The baby's dress is white with sheer lace around the very wide neck. It flares from the neck with no bodice or gathers. The little sleeves are caught up with blue bows at the shoulders. The bonnet has a sheer crisp frill around the face with blue ties and a blue bow on top. He wears little blue shoes and a two-strand necklace of amber beads.

Figure 213

1830s

America had a President from a frontier state—Andrew Jackson from Tennessee. He epitomized the frontier ideal—proud, courageous, and daring.

The great shipping age was in full swing in the East while rivers and canals were bustling with traffic. Spectators watched a demonstration of a new railroad steam engine—the transportation of the future.

Victoria became queen of England in 1837. In the United States girls' seminaries flourished, with some of the girls going on to the new colleges for women.

There was such a variety of coats for men at this time that styles overlapped and merged. With the more remote areas slower to receive new styles and rural areas tending to hold onto older ones, one might see many styles of clothing at any one time. The clothes of Figures 173, 184, 185, 199, and 200 were still being worn into the 30s as newer styles were appearing.

The coat was still tight-fitting and usually double-breasted. This man wears a new coat with the armholes and sleeves more fitted than in recent years with little or no fullness gathered in. The sleeves come just to the wrists; they no longer fall down over the hands.

The bodice is longer than a few years ago. It comes a little below the waist now and then rounds over the hips before forming the long tails. The tails are square instead of rounded. Most interesting of all are the lapels with notches or points where the collar meets the lapel. These notches were worn as early as 1815 and would still appear on coats in the 40s but most were worn in the 30s. The buttons are closer together at the waist and wider apart as they go up the chest to give the illusion of a small waist.

The cravat is tied in a bow now. Black ones were worn at times and red ones occasionally. White satin cravats were worn for formal wear. His shirt is tucked in the front with the edge of his vest showing at the coat neckline.

Pantaloon trousers were loose around the hips and had a high waist. They were stretched between suspenders at the waist and a strap under the foot to form a sleek line.

This gentleman wears the newly invented shiny silk hat which was not really silk but beaver processed in a new way. He carries a walking stick with a tassel hanging from the handle. Spurs were fashionable, too, even in the city!

Dark blue and black coats were worn for formal dress while dark green, mulberry, brown, black, and blue were worn for daytime. Pantaloons were made of corduroy, twilled textures, and small checks and stripes.

By the middle of the 30s collars became stiff and separate from the shirt. The dickey or false shirt was worn for the first time.

Figure 214

Miners, farmers, trappers, lumbermen, and stockmen who went through the Cumberland Gap into the wilderness were often pictured in coats that were loose and straight. Most had collars and lapels but some were collarless. Many were quite limp and they varied in length, most of them being the length shown here.

The pantaloons were usually very loose. Some appear to have been made of canvas or denim. Some men tucked the pantaloons into the boots while others rolled them up or wore them loose as shown. This man wears suspenders under his vest on his high-waisted pantaloons.

His hat is the large hat which eventually became the cowboy hat as well as a military one. Men wore these in a variety of shapes as each man shaped his own through the years. He used it to drink out of, fan with, fan a fire with, for a pillow, and a dozen other things as the need arose. Men also wore the stocking cap, bandana, and fur cap at times.

He wears a checked vest with a satin back and a shirt with the collar open. These shirts were often in colors such as green, blue, or red, red being the favorite.

Men of the frontier often wore beards, especially when out in the forest for a time, then shaved when in town.

He wears riding boots, either the turn-down boots of Figure 201 or the Wellington boots, originally military, which have a front that comes up over the knee and a back lower in the bend of the leg (see Figures 163 and 186).

Men often started out in the forest with clothes like this but would eventually change to Indian or deerskin clothes and moccasins as their clothes and boots wore out.

Polish immigrants came to America at this time because of the Revolution in Poland. Many of them wore the cap of Figure 202 with these clothes.

Figure 215

Figure 216

The woodland Indians had worn very little fringe, if any, in the forests, but when they moved to the plains during the 18th and early 19th centuries they wore more and more of it on their clothes. It eventually became quite long and must have been a marvelous sight rippling in the breeze as the Indian raced on horseback across the plains. Long fringe was used for purely esthetic reasons because of the way it extends and accentuates even the slightest body movement.

The buckskin clothing of the mid-19th century developed from these Indian clothes and was a result of two hundred years of white and Indian cultures coming together and influencing each other.

The fringe across the chest forming a yoke was in imitation of the earlier large cape-like collar of the 18th century buckskins. It survives today in the shirt yoke. It developed into something quite decorative in the yoke of the western-style shirt and jacket.

One of the earliest deeply fringed costumes was the one of "old Gabe," Jim Bridger, who explored Yellowstone, the Rockies, and discovered Great Salt Lake. People thought him crazy when he told of geysers springing up every hour, bubbling mud pots, and a lake in which you couldn't sink!

The deerskin clothes with the very long fringe were not commonly worn until later in the century, but "old Gabe" saw the plains Indians during his travels at this time and he was one of the first to adopt their clothing.

Early American Costume

Elastic was invented in 1836 by Charles Goodyear, but was used only on shoes and for garters. The first machine-made hooks and eyes were being manufactured too.

The diagonal line on the bodice had become an outstanding feature by this time. Necklines were very wide, even down off the shoulder, with the shoulder line dropped onto the upper arm. The entire front of this woman's slightly high-waisted bodice is tucked in diagonals. The sleeves are gathered in with much fullness at the drop-shoulder line, then fan out into huge sleeves which narrow quickly at the lower arm. They are longer than the arm and wrinkle before falling down onto the hands. Some sleeves were much larger even than these!

The skirt still has fullness on the sides and back; the hem is two or three inches off the floor. Pantalets are worn underneath. The wide belt has a jeweled buckle. These dresses were almost always either brown, black, or dark blue.

This lady's kerchief is very important as are all collars, kerchiefs, and capelets now. It is a small white kerchief edged with lace and caught with a cameo in front. It is more like a collar than a kerchief. Over the plain kerchief she wears another slightly larger one of a sheer, delicate lace. The custom of wearing two kerchiefs goes back to the 18th century.

Not only do the collars and kerchiefs appear in most portraits of this time, but these sheer lacy bonnets were practically a national costume. They are all much the same except for the ribbon decorations and the patterns in the lace ruffles. Many, like that of Figure 208, have at least two large, sheer ruffles of lace around the face. This one has blue satin bows inside the ruffle next to the cheeks and large bow ties under the chin.

Her hair is parted in the middle and worn in a topknot similar to Figure 222 (right). The front, instead of being pulled down onto the cheeks, is fashioned into two large rolls on each side leaving the ears exposed.

Figure 217

Figure 218

This girl wears the new style, wider look.

The wide neckline comes to where the armhole line usually is with the armhole line, as a result, dropped down onto the upper arm, giving a horizontal look to the new dresses. This bodice is tucked horizontally over the entire front. The sleeves are huge but just to the elbow, where they end in a flounce. Long mitts or extra sleeves extend up under the large sleeves.

The neckline is filled in with a sheer fabric which goes up to the neck, where a ruff or "betsy" is worn. Sometimes these ruffs were double or triple. Occasionally the neck was left bare and only the betsy worn.

The bonnet with its sheer two or three ruffles is extremely popular. Large pink satin bows decorate the top. The ties are curled on the ends, a custom which was continued for several years. Ribbons were dipped in milk, then wound around a broomstick till dry to form curls.

Many of the skirts of the period were quite plain. They had fullness in the back and on the sides, which were pleated. Wide belts often had jeweled buckles.

This dress in a plain cloth, without the mitts, was worn by mill girls. The apron of Figure 222 was worn over it.

Lovely imported shawls from India and fans and silks from the Orient were just a few of the things available as a result of the great shipping age and increasing trade with China and the Far East.

Ladies wore dresses with high but very wide, even off-the-shoulder necklines with diagonal lines across the bodice. The waistline was still a little above the natural waistline and skirt fullness was in the back and sides. Sleeves were still huge above the elbow. The satin bands on this lady's bodice begin at the waistline, cross, and extend to the shoulders, where they end in large bows, giving a very horizontal look. The belt is of the same satin. The cuffs are lace; the neckline is edged with a narrow lace ruffle.

The skirt, still about two inches off the floor, is worn over a hoop. She wears long pantalets underneath like those of Figures 223 and 224. Decorations around the hem were still elaborate like this wide lace flounce with two rows of ruchings. Pale blue checked gingham was fashionable as was solid red. Her stole, which is extremely important fashion-wise, is cashmere with a paisley design.

Her wide straw hat is decorated with large bows on the underside of the brim. The hat is bound with the same satin as the bows on the dress and adorned with several feathers and plumes.

Her hair is parted in the middle and pulled to each side in bunches of frizzed curls.

Figure 219

Figure 220

The very latest fashion was one of cleanliness. The custom of daily bathing was taken up by fashionable ladies and men.

Checked ginghams and plaids were very popular for dresses as well as dark colors such as brown and black.

The waistline was moving down toward the natural waist again but sleeves reached enormous proportions before the end of the 30s. They had to be stuffed with wicker frames or small feather pillows to hold them out!

Collars have grown so wide they now fall over the sleeves in a diagonal sloping line. This one has a little stand-up collar of its own and a large bow at the neck. A smaller collar squared at the shoulder line is shown in Figure 221.

Wide belts were still worn as were flat heel shoes.

Hair was worn in a topknot. A part from ear to ear divides the front hair from that in the topknot. The front section is then parted in the middle. Sometimes the sides are curled and held with combs as in Figure 209. This lady wears hers combed down onto the cheeks and then looped back up over the ears.

147

Early American Costume

Large capes, gathered at the neckline to form a rounded shape, were fashionable. They often had one or two small capelets around the shoulders. Slits were made for the arms to come through. These capes were often of wool and trimmed with bands of velvet. Formal ones were velvet with bands of satin or fur with fur collars. Fur muffs were worn as in Figure 195.

Her bonnet has a very large brim in front which becomes narrow in the center back with the crown slanted because the back part is deeper than the front. It is decorated with ribbons and plumes.

Figure 221

Working girls and women at home used aprons of bright or dark colors. They had the same wide neck as the dresses, only lower so the dress showed above. They buttoned or tied in the back just to the waistline and were open at the skirt. They were worn not only for work but for picnics and out of doors.

The woman on the left wears her hair in a knot or bun on the back of the head instead of on top. The front section is parted in the middle, combed down along the cheeks, then curved back under the ears.

On each sleeve at the wrist she wears a ribbon with a brooch on it to hold her sleeves in place.

On the right is a cape-stole which was seen in many, many variations. Some were small, others were very wide and as long in front as the dress. Small sheer, lacy ones were worn for summer. In winter they were wool or fur with a matching muff. Some were edged with fur but all were shaped much the same.

The hair of the woman on the right is combed in front in two large rolls over each ear with the ears exposed. The back is pulled up and wound around a large fan comb.

These aprons and stoles make dramatic costume changes without actually changing the dress.

Figure 222

1830-1840

Figure 223

Young girls still dressed like their mothers with wide, off-the-shoulder necklines and high waists. A young girl on the left wears a gathered bodice with full sleeves which taper to the lower arm. The sleeves are held in place with red ribbons and brooches around her wrists. On the neckline ruffle is a brooch which matches those on her wrist ribbons. The dress is unbleached muslin or tan wool.

Her skirt is gathered all the way around with several tucks around the hem and a row of tiny lace on the edge. Her pantalets have the same edging.

The cord around her neck holds a locket or miniature portrait. Sometimes the cord held scissors, a pin cushion, or trinkets needed for doing needlework samplers. (Women wore a monocle or pince-nez in this manner.) Even very young girls wore this cord, chain, or beads tucked into the bodice. They were tucked into belts, necklines, and under the bodice point.

Her hair is parted in the middle with curls pulled back exposing the ears.

The young girl on the right wears a dress with the same bodice and skirt but with a plain neckline and short, straight sleeves. It is a red plaid cotton trimmed with dark red braid. It is either a summer dress or one from a southern state.

Her hair is cut short and combed forward in the fashion of a few years ago.

Both girls wear the red shoes favored by many children at this time.

Little girls' clothes imitated their mothers' with the same enormous sleeves. On the left, a soft blue dress has rust-colored piping at the neckline and around the hem on the skirt. The belt is rust also. The ruffle around the neck is white lace.

The bodice is pleated around the neckline and the pleats are drawn to the center of the waistline, giving the popular diagonal line used on women's dresses. The sleeves droop down below the sleeve band at the elbow. They are stuffed with small feather pillows. She wears several petticoats to give the same fullness that her mother's hoop does.

She wears pantalets and rust-colored slippers with ties that cross over at the instep and tie around the ankle.

Her hair is pulled back severely into a knot or bun at the back, exposing the ears.

Her straw bonnet with its wide rust satin ribbons is similar to that of Figure 192. She wears red beads and carries a folding fan.

The little dress on the right appeared often with few variations. The bodice is tucked across the front and the neckline is so wide that it is off the shoulders. The waistband is quite wide, the skirt very full, and worn over several petticoats.

She wears lacy pantalets and an apron.

Similar dresses were red with black piping at the neckline and below the bosom. Another combination was a tan dress with black lace trim at the sleeves and around the neck and a sheer black apron trimmed with black lace. This one is beige calico with rust print leaves and rust piping trim with a black apron.

She wears rust shoes. Her beads are amber. Her hair is parted in the middle and pulled behind the ears.

Figure 224

149

Early American Costume

This little girl's simple muslin dress has a high waistline, full skirt, and large sleeves like those of adults. She wears long pantalets and high-topped red shoes.

Her hair is cut short and brushed forward in the adult style of a few years earlier. Little girls were often dressed in "old fashioned" clothes.

The baby wears a high-waisted dress of muslin with small puffed sleeves, a very wide neckline, and a long skirt. The cap has a crisp ruffle around her face with a red bow. She wears red beads around her neck like the little girl.

Figure 225

1840s

Hundreds of thousands of German immigrants came to America because of the German revolutions while thousands more came from Ireland because of the potato famine. Many were farmers, cotters, and laborers, but all classes of people were represented in all these groups.

The Mormons migrated to Iowa and Utah in 1847 and gold was discovered in California in 1848.

A new machine was invented for making felt, which created interest in new hat styles. In a very few years one would be a Stetson hat which would be known to most people as the cowboy hat.

The moustache, which had been adopted only by cavalrymen in recent years, now for the first time in a century was worn by gentlemen such as this one. His sideburns come down onto the cheeks and chin to become side whiskers.

Knee-length, tight-fitting coats with full skirts came into fashion in the 40s. This man's collar stands up in back, his sleeves are fitted, and there is no longer fullness at the shoulder line. Blue and gray were popular colors as were plaids and checks.

Vests were brocade, embroidered, or sometimes striped with turn-back lapels. The shirt collar points stand up above the black cravat, which is tied in a bow.

Trousers no longer had the front flap but instead had a button front closing sometimes with the buttons showing. The fly front was already being worn in Europe. Strap trousers were still worn but the latest fashions had a shaped hem which was longer in back than in front where it curved up over the foot. The back almost touched the floor. They were still loose in the thighs and hips, tapering to the ankle. Stripes and plaids of blue or gray and white were fashionable. White pique was worn in summer.

Watch fobs were still worn. The large straw hat was very popular, especially in the southern areas and around the Mississippi and Missouri rivers. It would be seen a great deal in the coming years along with the new felt ones.

Figure 226

Morning jackets and dressing gowns were of exotic designs and fabrics in paisleys or stripes. They were worn over trousers or pantaloons, shirt, and slippers, with a fringed cravat or scarf around the neck.

Rounded corners were new and this dressing gown has many of them. The splits in the side seams and sleeves are all edged with dark braid.

This gentleman wears a cord belt with tassels which is wrapped around the waist several times and tied.

His slippers are exotic, too, with their pointed toes. His cap is topped with a tassel at the crown.

He wears the new moustache with his short beard and curly hair covering his ears.

Figure 227

Figure 228

The United States had a war with Mexico in 1846. The uniforms from this war were to become the uniform of the West Point cadets into the late 20th century. The trousers were the straight fitted trousers which would be worn for well over a hundred years.

Infantrymen wore pale blue trousers and a jacket with white trim on the stand-up collar. Their dark blue cap had a chin strap. The brass belt buckle on the white belt and the plate on the white shoulder strap bore the Union initials and eagle.

Officers wore pale blue trousers and a dark blue jacket with yellow braid trim on collar, cuffs, and down the front edge. The uniform of corporals, sergeants, and higher officers had a yellow stripe down the trouser seams.

151

Early American Costume

This transitional-style dress of calico has the characteristics of the new dresses of the 40s but with the shorter length and flat-heel slippers of the 30s. The neckline is very wide and decorated with a sheer lace ruffle. The corseted bodice comes to a point in front. It is apparently separate from the full skirt, at least in front. There is a seam down the center front of the bodice with fullness pleated in at the bosom, which then drapes up to the shoulder line. Sleeve fullness has dropped suddenly to the lower arm with rows of shirring at the upper arm. Shirring is a characteristic of dresses of the 40s appearing over and over again. Sometimes black ribbons were tied around the sleeves at the wrists.

This woman wears a monocle or a pince-nez (eyeglasses) on a long chain, (ribbon, or beads) around her neck. Sometimes a locket or a miniature portrait or sewing implement was hung from the chain or ribbon. The bodice point apparently is separate from the skirt in front and it probably is a monocle or pince-nez that is tucked inside lest it swing against something and break.

The hair style still covers the cheeks but the knot or bun is lowered, like the sleeve fullness.

Figure 229

Figure 230

Plaids and checks were fashionable, possibly as a result of the great numbers of Scotch and Irish emigrants coming to the United States. Plaid taffetas were especially popular for formals, with plaid and check cottons for daytime. This dress is so simple and versatile that it can be made in almost any of the fabrics of the 40s such as muslin, linen, calico, or wool. Plaids of predominantly reds or greens were most popular.

The bodice is straight at the waistline like dresses of the 30s but is floor-length like the newest styles. The neckline is wide and low with a narrow self-binding which is repeated at the waistline seam. The short sleeves are made of two scalloped ruffles, one on the edge of a straight sleeve and the other sewn in with the sleeve at the armhole.

The scalloped edge of the sleeve ruffles, which is buttonhole-stitched, is repeated around the lower skirt. This dress can have a flounce around the hem like that of Figure 232 to match the sleeves.

Artificial flowers were becoming fashionable for the hair, dresses, and bonnets as shown here. The straw bonnet is flared at the front over a hair style like that of Figure 232.

The Mormons started to Iowa and Utah in 1847 in wagons, ox carts, and on foot. Some of the women wore plain dresses like this one with shawls and bonnets like those of Figures 192, 193, and 231.

152

1840-1850

Shirring and "V" design bodices were seen everywhere during this period. Sometimes the bands of shirring alternated with bands of plain cloth as on this bodice. The high neck has a lace collar and a large bow. The sleeves are shirred all the way to the wrists, where they have lace cuffs to match the collar.

The bodice comes to a point in front. Often these skirts were sewn to the bodice in back but had just a drawstring or waistband across the front which fastened on one side up under the boned bodice front.

The full skirt is worn over a hoop and several petticoats. Sometimes bands of shirring like those of Figure 233 decorate the skirt.

The lady wears a triangular shawl, the favorite wrap of the period. Shawls were of cashmere, silk, lace, embroidered, or India cotton. Some had fringe, some had ruffles or lace, and many had printed borders. Some were half circles, others were folded squares or circles.

Her bonnet is similar to Figure 230, only the crown is slightly higher. Older ladies still wore the bonnets of Figures 217 and 218 as well as the kerchiefs over black dresses.

Browns, rusts, tans, and black were important colors of the period.

Figure 231

Shirring became more complex toward the end of the decade. This bodice is shirred in at the point, waistline, and midriff, then releases the fullness below the breasts. The fullness is caught into gathers at the neckline with a binding. The same binding or cording is used at the edge of the bodice at the waistline. The front of the bodice is not sewn to the skirt (see Figure 231).

The upper sleeves are snug-fitting of plain cloth, then have three rows of shirring before ending in a ruffle above a full lower sleeve. This lower sleeve which is sewn under the ruffle is shirred in to fit the wrist. The shirring is only on the sides and underside of the wrist; the top is left plain with a point over the hand.

The full skirt, over hoop and petticoats, has bands of shirring and a flounce around the hem.

This dress might have been made from one of the newer paper patterns which were selling by the thousands through one New York pattern company. The tape measure had been invented too, resulting in better-fitting clothes.

Her hair is parted in the middle all the way down to the neck in back, then brought to each side in bunches of long curls. Sometimes artificial or fresh flowers were worn on each side or in a wreath around the crown.

Figure 232

Morning dresses or dressing gowns were a relief from the tight corsets. This one crosses over in front where it is held with a belt and hooks underneath. The neckline, front, and hem are edged with a band of shirring. The sleeves are shirred at the upper arm where they fit closely, then become large at the lower arm, and fit snugly at the wrist. Ruffles with pinked edges are used where the upper and lower sleeves meet.

The wide belt has a jeweled buckle. The bonnet is quite old-fashioned with its lappets (see Figure 76). These bonnets were only used indoors as lingerie caps at this time except by older women who still wore them with their black dresses. Her hair is like that of Figure 232.

Sometimes ladies wore mitts or gloves in the house with these dressing gowns in the mornings, even while doing embroidery!

Petticoats were worn underneath. These gowns were made in velvet for winter, sometimes with satin trim. Some were wool or taffeta with velvet trim. Many different trims such as ruchings, puffs, ruffles, cordings, and scallops were used.

Figure 233

Figure 234

This formal gown is important because it so accurately predicts the styles to come in the 50s and 60s. Machine-made lace could now be purchased by the yard; so it is extremely fashionable. Although at first glance it appears to have three tiers in the skirt, the dress actually only has two. The top tier is long and has a row of ruching about midway of its length. The bottom tier is longer in back so that it forms a train.

One dress of the period had black lace over yellow taffeta with black lace mitts. A very beautiful one was pale green satin with sheer white lace. White over red was a popular color combination as well as black lace over pink.

The lady wears flowers on the side of the bun of hair. This knot or bun has moved down the back of the head and onto the neck.

154

Figure 235

This girl's costume imitates that of Figure 229 even to the locket tucked under her bodice.

The calico dress of tan with rust and green flowers has a wide, off-the-shoulder neckline and is seamed down the front with extra fullness pleated in at the bosom. This fullness is taken to the shoulder for a diagonal line. The sleeves have two rows of shirring at the upper arms, then become full at a higher point than on women's dresses. They are longer than the arms so they pucker at the wrists and fall down over the hands. Sometimes ribbons are tied around the wrists to hold the sleeves in place.

Her skirt comes to her calf with her long pantalets filling in the space between the skirt and flat slippers.

She wears beads around her neck with a locket which is tucked up under the bodice, which is separate from the skirt in front. See description of Figure 229. Her beads are wound all the way around her neck once before hanging long in front.

Her hair is parted in the middle and pulled back.

A young boy wears the short jacket which originally was worn by sailors, then by revolutionists in France, and then by boys of all ages (see Figure 189). He is quite elegant with his vest with lapels and his black cravat. His trousers are striped and come just to the ankles above black slippers.

His coat is dark blue, the vest is gray-beige, and his trousers gray-striped.

His hair is combed in the very latest style with a side part.

Figure 236

Little boys wore tunics and smocks like those of European factory workers and peasants. The boy on the left wears a dark blue tunic with black braid trim. Its fullness is held in place by a cord with tassels tied around his waist. His chemise (underneath) has a ruffle at the high neck and long sleeves like those of women.

He wears white pantalets and his black shoes are high-tops. His cap is like those of Russia or Poland.

The little boy on the right wears a dress of small blue-and-white plaid. It has an off-the-shoulder neckline with piping trim. The same piping trims the pointed cuffs and the seams of the bodice.

His pantalets have two rows of tucks around the hem. Both the skirt and the pantalets are shorter than those worn by little girls.

His high-top shoes are bright red. His large sailor hat is straw with a navy blue ribbon band. He, too, wears the very new side part in his short hair.

Figure 237

Figure 238

The little girl's dress is muslin with rows of lace around the hem of its full skirt. It has puff sleeves. The neck is wide and has a drawstring as does the high waist. It ties in back. She wears a black apron for play, but white, gray, and brown aprons are worn as well. Her pantalets are lace-trimmed.

Her hair is parted in the middle and held in bunches of curls on each side with bows.

The baby on the chair wears a pale blue dress with an off-the-shoulder neckline. The bodice is full and gathered into a waistband at the natural waistline. The skirt is floor-length. The straight sleeves have a pleated ruffle at the elbow and another halfway between that and the shoulder.

His fine, soft hair is brushed straight back.

Both the baby and the little girl wear the popular bright red, high-top shoes.

CHAPTER 8

Constructing the Costumes

READ THE SCRIPT

Make notes as you read the script and underline with a bright color pencil any references to character or looks or clothing anywhere in it.

Also mark references to physical things such as "She placed the key in her apron pocket," or "He stuffed the map into his doublet," or "She grabbed his coat and pulled him back." Make a list for each character and jot these down as you go. When you begin your design this list will tell you what the costume must do such as have a pocket, a place inside for a map, or be able to withstand being pulled during rehearsal and performances.

Include in the list any reference to character as well. It is surprising how much this list will help you in designing and constructing each costume. If in the script a character has to fall or fight you must take this into consideration. A costume for a person who dances will have to be made with this in mind.

If you know in what period your play is set, if you analyze the physical needs of each character, and if you know what kind of person each is, you have done half the job.

Most materials, especially cloth, cardboard, felt, and foam rubber can be manipulated into almost any shape you need. You just have to get over your inhibitions—don't let the materials or the problems intimidate you. Start with the principle of expansion and contraction in mind and go from there as demonstrated on the how-to pages. All you need with the materials are scissors, pins, needle and thread, white liquid glue, paper, muslin, and your sewing machine. (Newspaper ad sheets will substitute for brown paper and old worn-out sheets will substitute for muslin.)

The following directions are not intended to be complete, but only an introduction to the various methods and materials you can use.

Be sure to label and file any patterns you make so that you can use them again. File your patterns by "sleeves, skirts, bodice, etc.," rather than by period or style. If you use this method you will acquire a more complete file using less space than if you file by costume, and you can find what you want more quickly, too.

Always baste hems until after dress rehearsal—when you and the director *know* it is right; then sew the hem on the machine. Never handsew hems, especially those of long skirts and coats. It can ruin the looks of the costume and the mood of the scene but it can be a physical danger as well to an actor when a ripped hem causes a fall. With dancers or characters who must be very active physically, you may need gussets sewn where the underarm and sleeve seams come together.

Always sew more than once over places of stress, but only when you are certain the garment fits and the director has given a final approval.

ZIPPERS

If you sew a hook and eye at the waist and at the neckline under the zipper, it will take the strain off the zipper and possibly prevent an accident during the play on the costume of a physically active character or one who wears a particularly tight-fitting costume. Even if a zipper should break during a scene these two hooks will hold the costume in place. But having a zipper break during the play is extremely unlikely if the hook and eye are used at the points of stress.

Actors, especially, like the hooks and eyes at the waist and neck because it makes dressing easier. When the hooks are fastened, the zipper glides right up easily and there's less danger of getting something caught in it.

Speaking of jamming the zipper, it is most important that you secure the fabric which is turned back under the zipper, particularly at the waistline. Stitch it down well so that it can't get in the way. I've seen actors in tears or temper tantrums just minutes or seconds before a cue during a quick costume change because the turned-back seam under the zipper was caught in the zipper. It should not be allowed to happen when a few minutes sewing can prevent it. I remember well in one play when this happened. The neckline hook was fastened as well as the waistline hook so the actress just went on stage with the back zipper open from the waist up and no one but those of us backstage knew the difference. But I learned my lesson well! I learned, first that a zipper must not be allowed to fail, and, second, if it should fail two hooks and eyes can save the day

It will give an actor or actress an extra feeling of security if you pin a safety pin to an inside seam somewhere to be used in case of emergency. When seconds count and some unforeseen accident happens (like catching a skirt on a piece of scenery) that pin might well save the day when there isn't time to run to the dressing room.

Zippers—To Have or Not To Have They are a fact of life and of the theatre, too. A costume should never have to be put on over the head unless it is so loose that it can be done with absolute ease. Why? First of all, the make-up and hair should be completed before the costume is put on. You have to experience only once the trauma of seeing an actor spill black eye make-up on the front of a white costume to understand why! Aside from accidents, this way of dressing is hard on a costume because it wrinkles and strains it around the armholes.

But even when accidents don't happen it can ruin a costume by smearing make-up around the neckline. If it doesn't ruin the costume it does ruin the make-up and hair style to pull on a tight costume over one's head. So use *long* zippers, 22" or 24" or even longer. Use them in the back or front instead of in the side seam. Make sure that the actor can be completely made up first and then step into the costume with ease. Remember that the actor is under a great deal of tension during the make-up and dressing session and that you, the designer, can help to ensure that he or she is as calm and relaxed as circumstances allow.

BUTTONS

Women wore no buttons until the 19th century except on very rare occasions.

Buttons in the 17th century were tin, lead, wood, brass, copper, and occasionally silver. They were frowned upon by the Puritans as a sign of vanity although only the most devout church members gave them up entirely.

In the 18th century they might be steel, pewer, pearl (last half of century), ivory, cloth-covered, or stitched wood. The stitched wood was done by sewing through a series of tiny holes in the button to form decorative patterns. This stitching probably served to strengthen the button as well as decorate it.

Metals were used in the 19th century as in earlier years. Buttons became very decorative and experimental. They were made of glass, porcelain, and even paper (probably papier-mâche). They were crochet-covered wood, hand painted (on a variety of materials), and jewelled. Sometimes they were jewelled with real gems! Button-making became both an industry and an art by the end of the century.

In theatre it is sometimes easiest to make a period costume fasten the way it actually did in historic times. This is especially true of coats. When a fabric doesn't have the strength or firmness to stand the wear or when a costume change must be made quickly it may be best to just sew buttons on for appearance and use a zipper or snaps for the real fastening.

Revolutionary soldiers replaced lost buttons with old cartridge balls covered with a bit of rag. They also used cartridge balls to weight their coattails to make them hang attractively—a very practical idea for theatre.

ACTORS' COMPLAINT

Actors' most often-voiced complaint is that a costume is restrictive or uncomfortable.

There are two schools of thought on this. This complaint comes from directors as often as actors because when the director complains to the actor that he or she is not interpreting the part as well as he should, the reply might be "I can't do it in this costume—it restricts my expression." A costume should fit properly and should not bind or chafe an actor.

A costume must be comfortable and certainly never painful but being *authentically restrictive* is something else altogether. *A good actor and a good director will learn something about the times they are dramatizing.* A performer should work within at least *some* of the restrictions that the real person (on whom the character is based) would have experienced. If you feel strongly about this, it might be a good idea to discuss it with the director and find out his or her feelings about it.

An actor should not have to be preoccupied with keeping something in place; it's not fair to him.

An actor or actress who is interpreting an 18th century person with the freedom of today's soft stretchable clothes, will interpret the part as a 20th century person if rehearsing in soft sweater and jeans.

All through history, and to a degree today, fashion has attempted to separate the classes. When new, fashion is expensive, but it is also restrictive when compared to functional work clothes.

In history an upper-class person would have worn clothes that allowed very little freedom of movement in order to show that he or she was upper-class. Also, an upper-class person simply did not *need* such flexible clothes since he (she) did little more than sit, stand, and walk rather stiffly. Bending, stretching, running, etc., were left to the peasants.

Actors Perspire

If you say this to most actors they will reply, "I don't perspire—I sweat!" By putting a drop of water on a sample of your cloth you can see if it is one of those pale colors which turn dark when wet. If it is, it is a good idea to sew in underarm pads—either those available in department and variety stores, which are expensive, or those you can make yourself. They don't have to be waterproof, just several layers of soft absorbent cloth. I was examining an 1880s dress in a museum collection several years ago and discovered to my surprise that it had underarm pads of the same fabric as the bodice sewn right in. There's very little that we can think of that hasn't been done before.

During a run a costume can become permanently discolored or damaged by perspiration. Some actresses get very upset over the stains so the underarm pads can help to give a feeling of security as well as preserve the costume. You as the designer will have to consider these factors and decide if a costume needs this protection.

ANALYZE THE DESIGN

The first step in making a costume after it has been designed is: *Be careful that you understand the design.* If it is calf-length, make it calf-length, not knee-length or ankle-length. This seems such a simple thing but *it is the most common mistake made by costumers.* It drives designers to fits of temper at times!

I've had people put gathers in sleeves when there should be none, make a waistline at the waist when the plate clearly shows it high or low-waisted, and men's coat lengths every way but the length the plate indicated.

This is why I have used human proportions for my drawings instead of the exaggerated fashion figure which

is attractive but can make it impossible for the person doing the sewing. It is possible to interpret the drawings in this book accurately because the calf, waistline, knee, etc., is where one expects it to be.

COLLARS, KERCHIEFS, AND SHAWLS

Men's Collars   The stand-up collars of Figures 161, 162, 163, 175, 189, and 190 had stiffening or boning in them to make them stand up; the best way to achieve that same look in a costume is to use a stiff interfacing.

Kerchiefs   The kerchief can be sewn to the dress if you don't want to have to arrange it for each performance. If you do this, first make the dress, then arrange the kerchief right on the dress on the actress, and baste it in place. Then sew it securely by hand. It will have to be cut in the center back and basted down along each side of the back zipper. It can be sewn securely by hand or machine later. It isn't complicated; the most important thing to do is to arrange it properly first and baste it in place. You may have to do this if that costume has to be put on in a quick change. It is not unusual for a change to have to be made in as little as two or three minutes. Sometimes a kerchief can be left tied or fastened and simply slipped on over the head. If you decide to do this, sew a snap on the kerchief and the dress and just slip it on and snap into place.

The following kerchiefs, falling bands, collars, and small shawls will increase your design possibilities. They are all taken from old portraits but the dresses underneath are the same as dresses already shown in the costume illustrations, and it would be repetitious to give them all.

17th and 18th Century

1. The Elizabethan fan collars, like those of Figures 20 and 22, and ruffs of Figures 7, 21, and 23, although stiffly starched, still required more support. Women wore these wire frames underneath to ensure that the collar didn't collapse.

2. Seventeenth-century falling bands for men and women should fall from high up on the neck if the costume is to have the proper period look.

First, use a neckband like those on a modern man's shirt and attach the falling band at the *top* as shown. Attach the ties and it is ready to get into easily. This is the way they were actually made.

3. The kerchief is pulled down behind the laces, then pulled out in a series of puffs graduating in size. It is worn modestly toward the neck, covering most of the bosom.

4. Two bows hold a kerchief which is curved so that it fits the shoulders and front of the bodice without folds and lies quite flat. A string of beads on a double ruffle is worn around the neck.

5. A small kerchief follows the neckline around to the front where it is tied much like a man's cravat with the ends hanging down.

6. This one is worn wide around the shoulders and tied in a bow at the front. Another similar one is caught

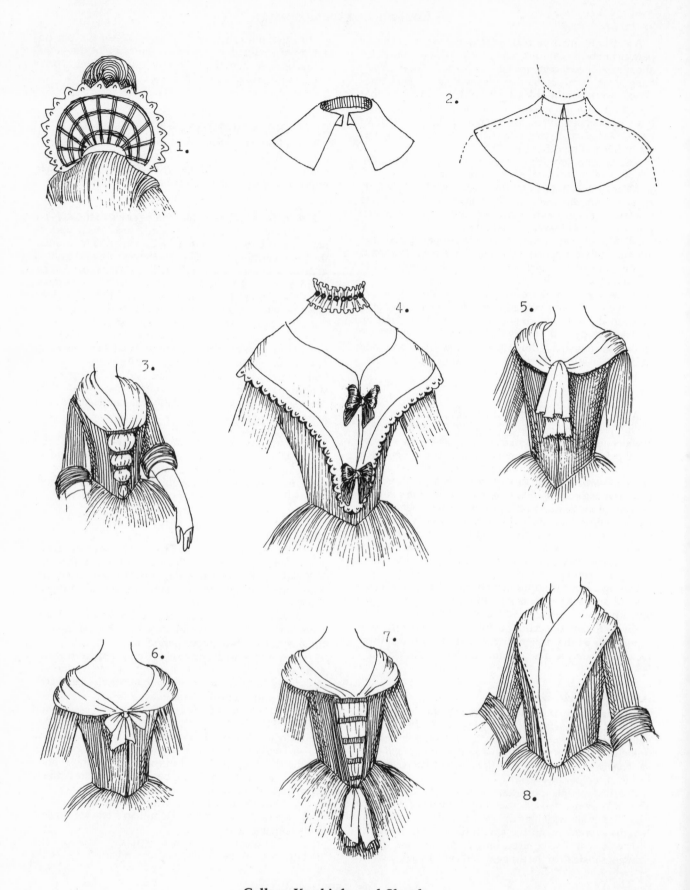

Collars, Kerchiefs, and Shawls

and tied with a satin ribbon with the ends of the kerchief tucked into the bodice.

7. A long kerchief is worn wide out on the shoulders and then behind the corset laces. It is flat with the ends hanging out below the corset point.

8. There is no sign of a pin or any fastener holding this kerchief which covers the entire bosom and even goes up high on the neck. It has obviously been carefully arranged in front and smoothed against the bodice till it is quite flat.

9. One artist carefully painted the tiny rolled hem and lace edge of this sheer kerchief as well as the pin holding the corner. A ribbon is pinned at the center front where the squared ends overlap.

10. This one is similar to Number 5, but modestly pulled up all the way to the neck where it is tied like a cravat. Aside from modesty, it might be pulled up around the neck for warmth.

11. A small black sheer kerchief is held in front by a brooch. The lace on the edges forms a dark border around it. It is a curved crescent shape with rounded front edges, much like that of Figure 165 but without a white one underneath.

12. A large sheer white kerchief is fastened at the waist, giving the appearance of a shawl.

13. A very large brooch holds a curved kerchief around the shoulders forming a bertha. The ends hang in front.

14. This one is similar to Number 8, but worn inside. It is overlapped so far in front that it comes up high on the neck, completely filling the neckline.

15. A very long narrow kerchief is worn wide, almost off the shoulders. It is tied like Number 5 with the long ends coming down to the knees.

16. Many portraits show the bodice front flaps open, exposing the corset lacings underneath. Several of these show the kerchiefs of Numbers 3 and 7 worn with it. Sometimes the corset was worn underneath, but often the bodice was boned so that it and the corset were one and the same.

19th Century

17. A very dainty black sheer scarf hangs loosely around the shoulders, perhaps pinned at the corner of the wide neckline. A ruffle and beads are worn around the neck.

18. This style kerchief appears in a number of portraits. It is overlapped and sewn in front with an edge of lace all the way around. It has to be slipped on over the head.

19. Plaid and paisley scarves were immensely popular at this time. This long plaid one goes around the neck, crosses over the bosom and then back to the rear where it is tied in a bow. The shoulder button of Figure 197 would be particularly useful for this kerchief.

20. Almost like a collar itself with its rounded corners and neat hem, this kerchief comes down to the Empire waistline where it is fastened with a bow. Its lace collar is like that of Figure 208 but is attached to the kerchief instead of the dress.

21. Boas were popular as well as shawls and stoles as in Figure 219. This one, instead of feathers, is made of yards and yards of gathered tulle which spirals a cord base. It can also be made of many circles of tulle gathered and threaded onto a cord or ribbon. It has satin bows on each end.

22. This large collar has its own small lace collar and a very full, crisp lace ruffle around the edge. It is held in front with a large cameo brooch.

23. A wonderfully practical idea appears in one portrait: buttons on the belt for holding a shawl in place!

24. The small shawl hanging loosely like this appears in enough portraits to indicate it was commonly worn. The huge sleeves prevent it from slipping off the shoulders. Such shawls appear in brown, blue, and orange-red, some with fringe, some plain.

25. A rust-colored shawl edged with lace is pulled up high around the neck and smoothed flat in front indicating modesty, old age, or just a cold room.

26. This long sheer kerchief is unusual in the way it comes to the bosom, then folds and goes toward the back. It is neatly hemmed on both sides and appears to fasten in back or is slipped on over the head, with its seam in back.

27. A tan shawl with a blue border and blue fringe is worn in an attitude between the casual one of Number 24 and the precisely arranged, modest one of Number 25. These three are excellent examples of how you can use the shawl to express the character of three different women or a change of character in one.

28. A "betsy" similar to that of Figure 218 has a wider neck like that of the dress of Figure 222. It is an embroidered sheer fabric with a lace ruffle constructed in the manner illustrated.

29. A triangular kerchief is worn around the shoulders under a smaller, rectangular one caught at the corners with a ribbon bow. Both are trimmed with lace ruffles. They might be sewn together so that the rectangular one forms a collar as shown in the diagram.

30. A dark dress with a high, very wide neckline has a sheer white collar as its only decoration. It is held together with a brooch and edged with narrow lace.

31. After machines were developed for making lace, large lace shawls in a variety of shapes were popular. This black sheer one, held together with a brooch, falls around the shoulders following the off-the-shoulder neckline of the dress.

Kerchiefs and shawls were cut in whatever shape would give the desired effect. Experiment with a few yards of thin muslin, batiste, or soft jersey to discover for yourself some of the interesting results you will get when you use some of the shapes diagrammed.

Diagram "f" is the shape you will need for long kerchiefs such as the ones in Figures 156, 164, and 176 and color plate Number 12. This elongated triangle gives a point in back but without bulk in front. They can also be created with the shapes of diagrams "d," "e," and "g". The kerchief in Figure 176 is an elongated triangle with the ruffle on the long straight side (the base of the triangle).

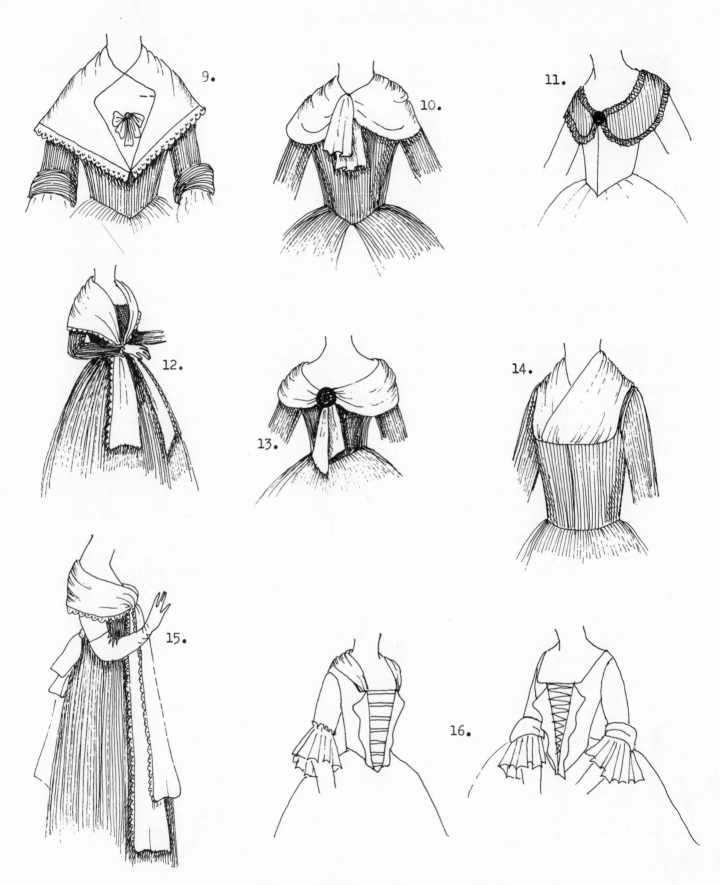

Collars, Kerchiefs, and Shawls (*continued*)

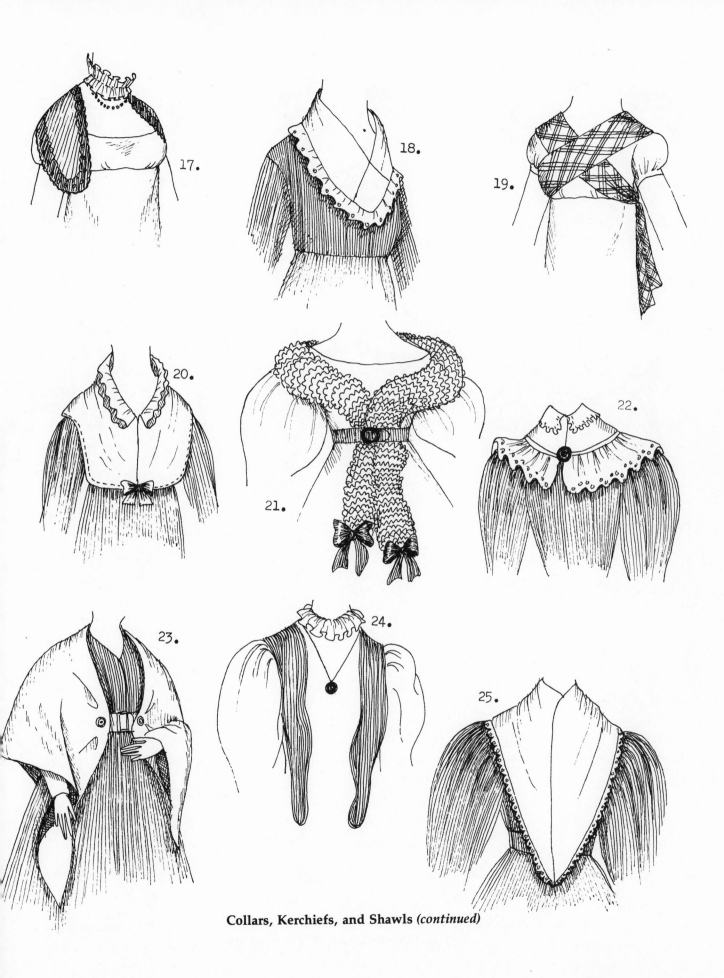

Collars, Kerchiefs, and Shawls (*continued*)

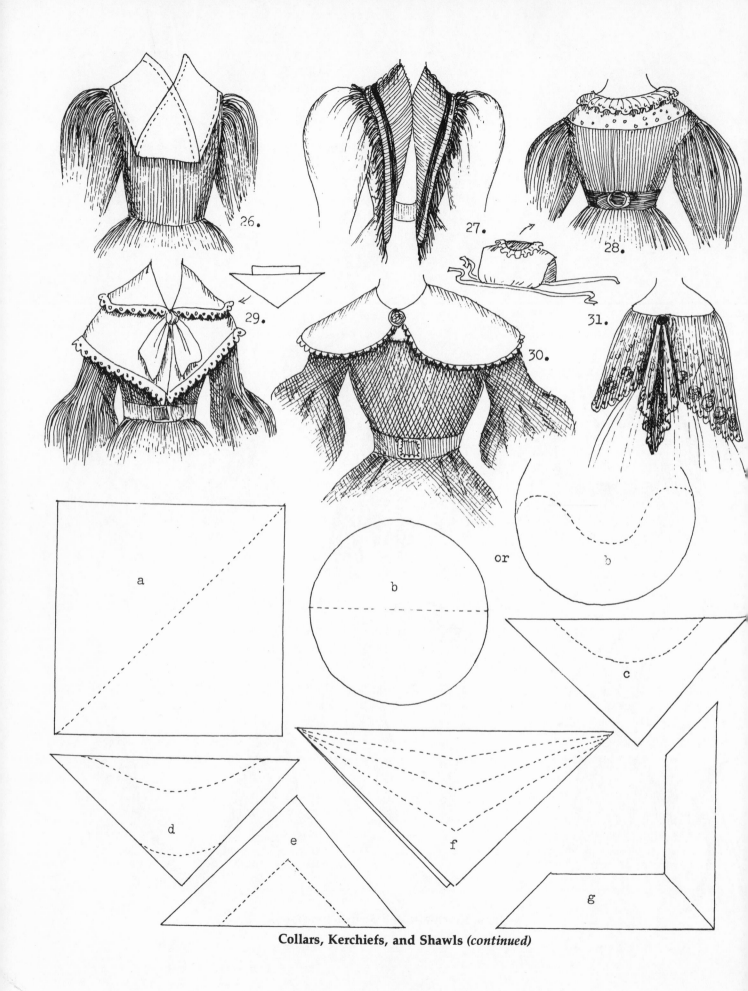

Collars, Kerchiefs, and Shawls (*continued*)

DRAPING THE SKIRT

In early colonial days (16th and 17th centuries) women had to pick up their skirts to get them out of the filth of the streets. Before long it was done in individual creative ways, then developed into fashion which continued into the 18th century. After the Revolution it was discontinued until the 1870s when it became high fashion again but in a more artificial way.

Many of these skirts had aprons either over or under the draped skirts. All the skirts shown appeared in paintings on dresses like those already shown. You can use any of the designs or perhaps become inspired by them and design your own. Almost anything we can think of today was probably tried at some time or other.

17th Century Skirts

1. The plain skirt is picked up at about the knees on each side, pulled up, and fastened under the bodice on each side. The result is the same when viewed from the front or the rear.

2. An open skirt has the corners of the skirt pulled up *underneath* and tucked under the corset. The corners can be twisted as they are pulled under to make the skirt puff out in panniers.

3. Catch the skirt at the hem on each side, then pull it up underneath to the waist, and fasten or tuck it. Several paintings show this at various lengths, so it apparently was not always pulled all the way to the waist but was fastened at different heights over the hips.

4. This skirt which is open in front has the corners pulled to the back on top of the skirt and tied in a small knot. (This can be done with the corners pulled under and tied underneath to give quite a different effect.)

5. This skirt is picked up at each knee, pulled up, and fastened across the waist in front.

6. A plain unopen skirt is picked up at mid-thigh in front and pulled snugly around the waist to the back where it is fastened.

7. The front of the skirt is caught a little above the knees, then pulled up underneath and fastened toward the back.

8. An open or divided skirt is picked up several inches above the corner on each side and pulled to the back at the hips where it is fastened and decorated with a bow. The skirt is pulled up so that it puffs out over its bottom edge instead of being folded up as in Number 12 to show the "wrong" side of the cloth.

Skirts were either tucked into the waist, which was usually a drawstring, or just tucked up under the bodice. The skirt will stay securely if the waist is tight. Pins were commonly used as were ribbon ties.

9. The front corners of a divided skirt with a train are pulled to the back. They are each pulled on around to the far side, crossing over each other in center back above the knees in a wrapping fashion.

10. The sides are picked up at the hem and carefully pulled up to the waist forming a swag in front. This is most effectively achieved by stitching up the side and drawing it up. (This is one of the styles later revived in the Victorian era of the 1870s, 1880s.)

11. This is almost the same as Number 3 with the hem of the skirt sides pulled up to the outside, exposing the back of the cloth instead of being pulled underneath. The skirt can be fastened at various heights.

12. The divided skirt is picked up several inches above the hem and folded up and over toward the back, exposing the back of the cloth. This and Numbers 9 and 11 are particularly attractive when a cloth is used that is different on the back, such as a brocade.

18th Century Skirts

13. The front corners of this divided skirt are pulled back underneath just slightly.

14. The corners of the skirt (and sometimes the sides at the hem) of this flowing robe are pulled in through the pocket slits of the panniers. Pockets are described in Figure 107.

15. A plain skirt is picked up at the hem on each side and pulled through the pocket slits. It is pulled in far enough to shorten the skirt in front and back.

16. A divided skirt is shirred up at each side of the back, making three swags as shown. Drawstrings were made in the skirt and it could then be drawn up to any height like Austrian curtains. It is decorated with satin ribbons.

17. This one is like Number 16 but drawn up once in the center back instead of at each side back. This, too, can be drawn up to any height.

18. This divided skirt has the front corners pulled up and under all the way to the center back at the waist, drawing it up high in the old 17th century manner.

THE BODICE

1. Start with a basic commercial fitted bodice pattern. Be sure it fits the actress who is to wear it.

2. Any style neck can be made from it such as the simple square necks of Figures 8 and 11. Make a paper pattern first, then make any needed adjustments before cutting a muslin pattern. Be sure to label the paper pattern as to size before you file it away.

3. A point can easily be made for the front. Be careful to look at the style you want since these points vary from very long and pointed to shallow or rounded.

4. The very low below-the-bosom necklines such as Figures 166 or 180 should have the darts basted in a muslin pattern before marking and cutting the neck. It should be marked right over a dress form or a person of the correct size.

5. The deep "V" necks such as those of Figures 90, 96, 118, or 131 should also have the darts basted first before marking and cutting.

6. Bodices can be made shorter-waisted, too, to any length needed.

7. The low-necked Empire bodices such as Figures 177, 179, 194, 196, 197, and 204 can be shortened at the waist or lowered at the neck to whatever degree needed.

8. When making a pattern for the gathered Empire bodices such as those of Figures 171, 191, 192, 193, or 197, first make a fitted bodice to be used as a lining in order to retain the proper form.

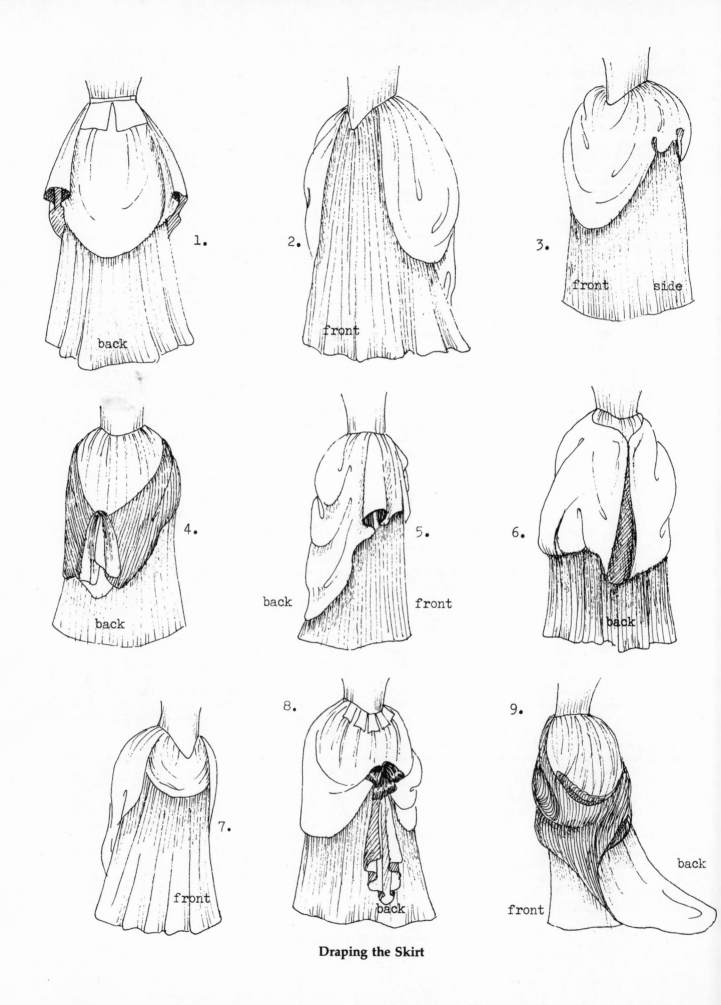

Draping the Skirt

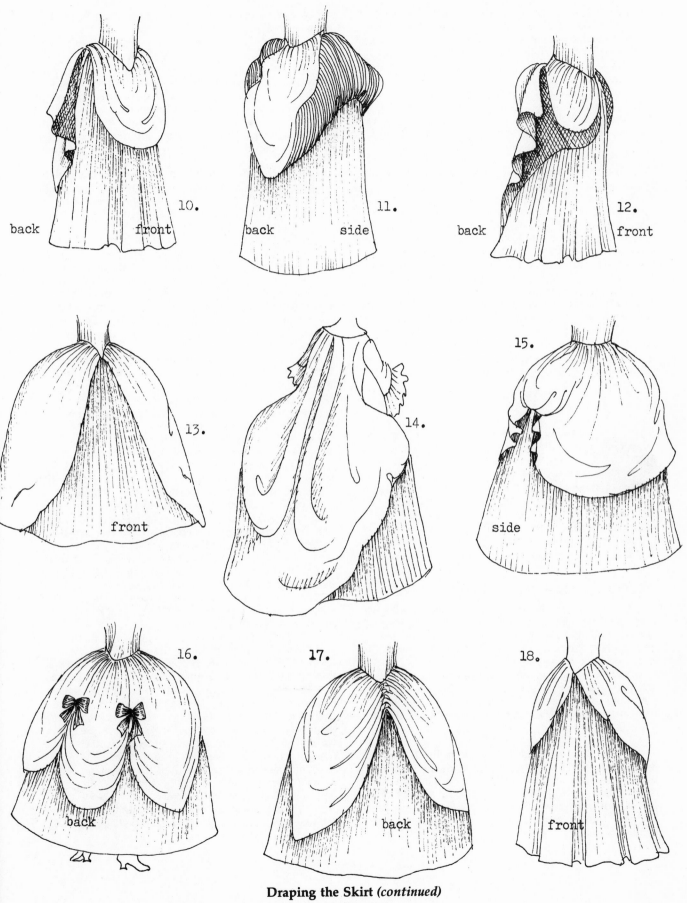

Draping the Skirt (*continued*)

9. After you have the lining or form pattern of Number 8, cut and spread it several inches, depending on the fullness needed and the size of the actress's bosom. Analyze the period style carefully since some styles are quite full while others are only slightly gathered. Gather to fit the lining.

10. The bodices of Figures 169 and 170 have both a natural waistline and an Empire line, too. Gather it to conform to a fitted lining. You may want to make another row of gathering between the Empire and natural waist.

11-a. The shirred bodice of Figure 232 should be made over a plain fitted bodice lining with a rounded point. Baste the darts. (This method can also be used for the child's bodice of Figure 224.)

11-b. Expand the bodice pattern 4" to 8" depending on the thickness of the fabric to be used for the dress. (The more delicate the fabric, the more fullness can be used.)

11-c. Stitch by hand from the *outside* edge of the waistline dart, across to the opposite line as shown. Make several rows approximately an inch apart. Use triple or quadruple thread thickness to ensure it staying intact. Leave thread ends loose.

Stitch across the neck, leaving the thread end loose. Place it on a dress form or person over the fitted lining of Number 11-a and draw up the threads until it conforms perfectly to the lining. Secure the thread ends and baste the lining and bodice together. Sew over the shirring and you are ready to sew it to the bodice back.

———

The draped bodice of Figure 229 is easiest when the drape over the bosom is simply added on top of a basic fitted bodice, basted, then sewn in place. This is true also of the shirred bodice of Figure 231.

A drop-shoulder can be made by extending the shoulder line about 2 inches. The tucked bodices of Figures 220, 221, 217, and 218 can best be made by sewing tucks in your fabric *before* cutting the bodice.

The shirred Empire bodice of Figure 178 should be made over a plain unshirred lining of the proper shape.

BREECHES, TROUSERS, AND LEGGINGS

1. For your permanent pattern file you should have men's and boy's shorts and long trousers in several sizes. For the trunk hose, sometimes called "Florentine hose," such as those of Figures 2, 3, 13, 14, and 26, start with the front and back of the pattern.

2. Draw a line on a piece of paper for the side seam and place the patterns several inches apart, fanning the pieces out so that they are further apart at the legs than at the waist as shown. Make darts at the waist and gather at the legs as shown.

3. For the authentic slashed hose of Figures 2, 3, 13, and 14, lay strips of braid, felt, or cloth directly onto a lining made by the directions under Number 2, starting with the center one first. Put this one on the line which approximates the side seam, then fan out several more just slightly as shown. Stitch them only at the waist and leg band, leaving them free in the middle so they resemble the old slashes. Gather the legs and waist on bands.

4. For a knee-length pattern cut trousers below the knee as shown.

5. For full petticoat breeches such as Figures 61, 65, 69, or 127, or full breeches such as Figure 17, 57, or 62, expand and fan out the knee-length pattern as shown. How much you pull them apart and how much you fan them at the bottom depends on which of these you want. They vary in fullness. Pleat at the waist.

The outer pair of petticoat breeches should be considerably fuller than the linen ones underneath. (Figure 127 wears the full outer breeches over 18th century knee breeches.)

6. For the large hipped breeches with slender thighs such as those of Figures 4, 5, or 15, fan the knee-length trousers pattern out at the waist, keeping them narrow at the knees as shown. Some fullness can be added or taken away at the inseam as shown.

7. For 18th century knee breeches, fan the pattern out at the waist a few inches as shown. Some fullness can be taken away at the knee by overlapping the outseam corners as shown. Measure the leg below the knee, add a little and make the bottom correspond to that measurement. Although knee breeches were snug in the thighs they were quite loose in the hips and seat. Dart in the waist to fit as shown. Cut off the corner of the center back as shown for the back laces.

The hem should curve to fit the knees when the leg is bent. Curve it down a little in front to add length and up in back to fit the bend of the leg as shown. Knee breeches should be only slightly gathered at the knee. If you need to take out fullness at the knee, take it from the inseam.

8. Breeches were not made very accurately because the tape measure was not even in existence at this time. They had, therefore, to be adjustable by lacings in back.

9. This diagram shows the front flap construction begun in mid-18th century and continued until the 1840s when the fly front became fashionable in Europe.

10. Collect modern (non-flared) trouser patterns in several sizes. You can make them with a side or outseam or join the front and back pieces as shown for a one-piece pattern. Make a dart at the side waist.

11. For the tapered trousers of Figure 226, fan the waist out to add fullness while overlapping the ankles to decrease the fullness as shown. The hem should be curved up in front and down in back as shown. This curved hem was very fashionable. The back should almost touch the floor.

12. The military trousers or leggings of Figure 148, and color plate Number 5, or the strapped trousers of Figures 199-left and 214, should have a slight curve although not as deep as Figure 226.

13. For Indian leggings with the front strap such as Figures 81, 82, or color plate Number 4, cut away pattern as shown. *Felt, when washed in hot water and run through the clothes dryer, looks surprisingly like real leather.* Be sure to wash the felt *before* cutting the leggings because it shrinks when washed. Fold over the strap for a belt casing.

The washed felt can be used for deerskin hunting shirts and coats and it fringes beautifully when clipped with a good sharp pair of scissors.

14. Use the washed felt described in Number 13 for the side-strap Indian leggings like those of Figures 34, 35, and 145, and color plates Number 1 and 7.

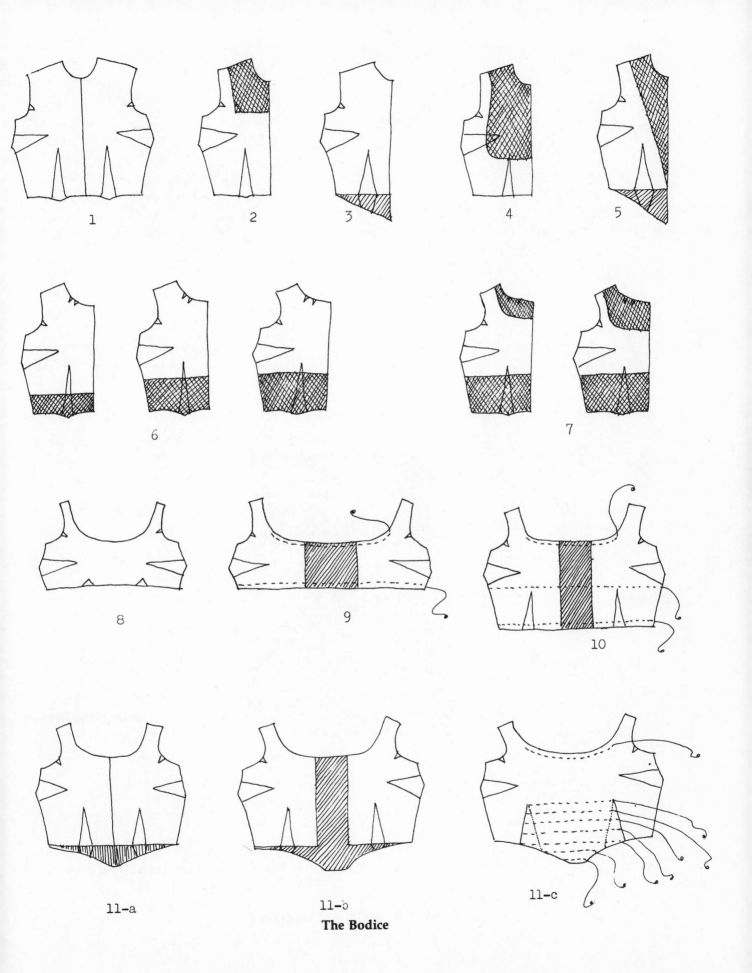

1

2

3

4

5

6

7

8

9

10

11-a

11-b

11-c

The Bodice

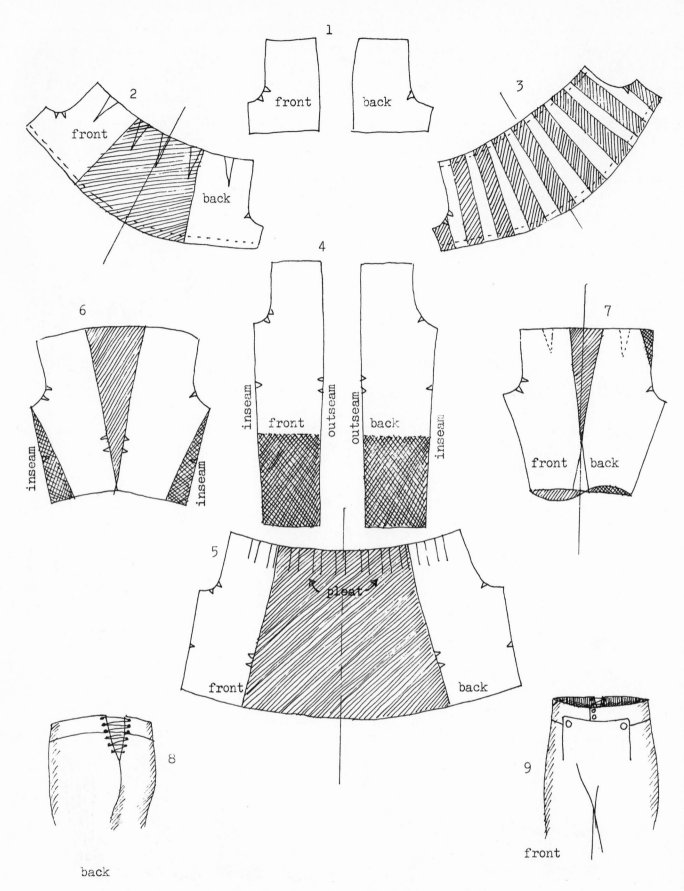

Breeches, Trousers, and Leggings

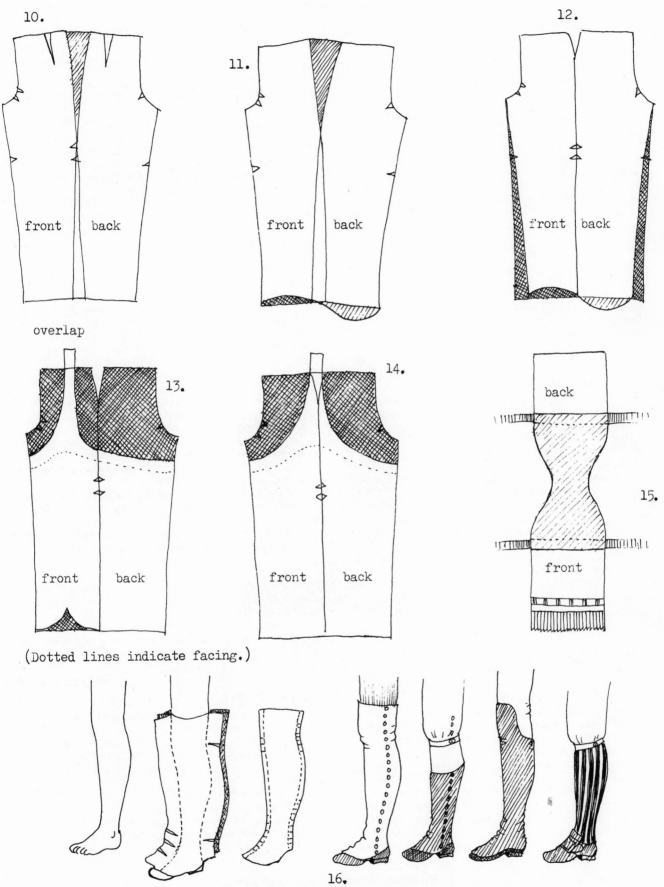

10.

front   back

11.

front   back

12.

front   back

overlap

13.

front   back

14.

front   back

back

15.

front

(Dotted lines indicate facing.)

16.

Breeches, Trousers, and Leggings *(continued)*

15. A felt Indian breechcloth should be curved in to fit the crotch. A contour diaper or woman's bikini bottom pattern can be used for a guide if you need one.

It should be lined with muslin in the center. The muslin can also provide the casings for the belt. The breechcloth hung down in back and front but was usually only decorated or fringed on the front flap.

I made leggings and breechcloths of washed felt for Nashville Children's Theatre's production of "Indian Captive" and several young men in the cast wore them for 30 performances. We assumed, modestly, that jockstraps under skin-colored tights would be a necessity, but on opening day I discovered to my surprise that all the actors and the director had decided during dress rehearsal that they weren't necessary. We had made the breechcloths modestly wide and the contoured shape fit so snugly that they never caused a single raised eyebrow.

Their success can be attributed to the well-designed shape and snug fit but also to the muslin lining which never allowed the felt to stretch.

16. Gaiters, military leggings, boots, and stockings can be made by pinning and then basting two pieces of muslin together down the center front and back of the leg as shown.

Clip the front at the curve of the foot as shown to prevent wrinkling. When the fit is perfect, but not tight, trim it to leave about ½ inch seam allowance and clip the curves at the ankle and the back of the knee as indicated.

Mark with a pencil along the basting lines, then take out the basting, and make a pattern from the pieces. Bonded vinyl works well for gaiters (sometimes called spatterdashes) but felt or cloth will work if lined. The vinyl needs no hemming anywhere.

Use a long separating zipper in the back seam to make dressing easier and quicker. If you want button gaiters like those of Figures 104, 143, 144, 148, 150 and others, it works best to put just buttons or studs down the side without a real opening. It takes too long to really button them each time and they have a tendency to gap between the buttons.

Put an elastic strap under the foot to hold the gaiter in place and give a snug fit.

17. Boots can be made by this method using bonded vinyl. Stockings such as the striped and plaid ones of Figures 128, 147, and 140 can be made by this method using knit or woven cloth cut on the bias.

SLEEVES

Use a basic sleeve pattern for a long fitted sleeve (no gathers at the armhole or wrist).

It is best if you use the plain basic fitted sleeve as a lining under the large sleeves with the outer, period sleeve secured to it. This will prevent its twisting, slipping, or losing its shape.

You can change the shape in any way you like by cutting the pattern horizontally or vertically as shown.

1. Most period sleeves either had seams in front or in both front and back. Most curved to conform to the arm. Men's coat sleeves are still made this way but with a little less curve.

Divide the basic sleeve pattern in half vertically, then

in quarters as in 1-a. Remove the two outside quarters and join them together at the original underarm seam as shown in 1-b and 1-c and you have the patterns for a front and back-seamed sleeve.

2. Curve these new outer and under sleeve sections by clipping them and expanding at the elbow as shown in 2-a and 2-b.

3. For a single seam at the front of the arm use the same principle as Number 1 but remove only a quarter of the sleeve from the front part to the back as in 3-a through 3-d, joining the pieces at the original underarm seam. The single-seam sleeve was used mostly for women and children in the 18th and 19th centuries.

4. The ruffles on women's 18th century dress and chemise sleeves hung gracefully because they were often cut longer in back than in front. They can be made from a crescent-shaped piece as in 4-a or from a circular piece with a circle cut from the center as shown in 4-b.

5. Divide and mark the basic pattern both vertically and horizontally as demonstrated in 5-a and 5-b.

6. By cutting on these lines, you can change the shape of a basic sleeve into any period sleeve. By cutting the vertical line halfway down and across the center horizontal line, you can spread the pattern to add fullness to the sleeve above the elbow. Keep the underarm seam intact, only spread from the inside as shown.

7. This demonstrates how you can increase the fullness by spreading the sections wider apart.

8. By cutting on other horizontal lines as shown you can curve the underarm seam as you spread it still wider, creating the extreme fullness of the sleeves of the 1830s.

9. This sleeve is spread to create the shape of the fashionable sleeves of the 1820s. It is also lengthened at the wrist by adding a piece to come down over the hands as in Figures 206, 207, and 208.

10. This sleeve has the fullness beginning ¾ of the way down instead of ½ way down as in Numbers 6 and 7 above.

11. In the 1840s the fullness was at the lower arm instead of the upper arm so the spreading is at the bottom.

12. This 17th century sleeve is not rounded much at the shoulder line and the whole sleeve is spread apart to create fullness. The wrist fullness should be darted instead of gathered.

13. A drop-shoulder shirt sleeve is spread apart vertically with the shoulder line lowered to compensate for the drop-shoulder of the shirt body.

MEN'S COATS

For period coats for men, you should have a basic bodice pattern in several sizes. A woman's bodice can be adjusted for a man by leaving off the darts, enlarging the armholes, and extending the shoulder line. Make a muslin bodice and baste and trim it right on a form or a person to perfect it.

Men's modern coat patterns can be used as a starting point and modified to period lines.

For many of the men's coats you can use a woman's coat pattern. Occasionally you will find them very similar in line. The main thing is to familiarize yourself with the

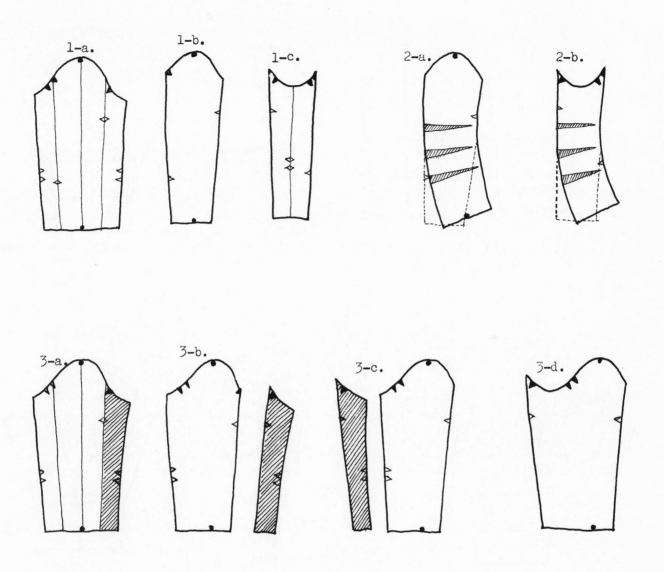

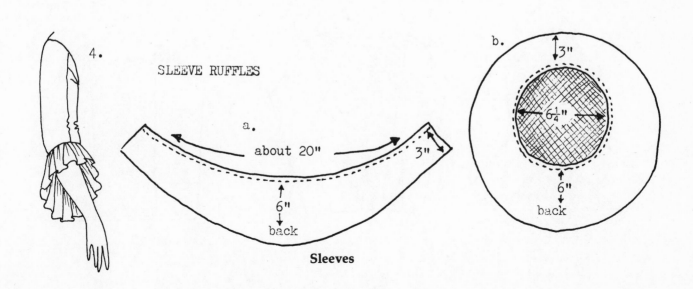

SLEEVE RUFFLES

about 20"

3"

6"

back

6$\frac{1}{4}$"

3"

6"

back

Sleeves

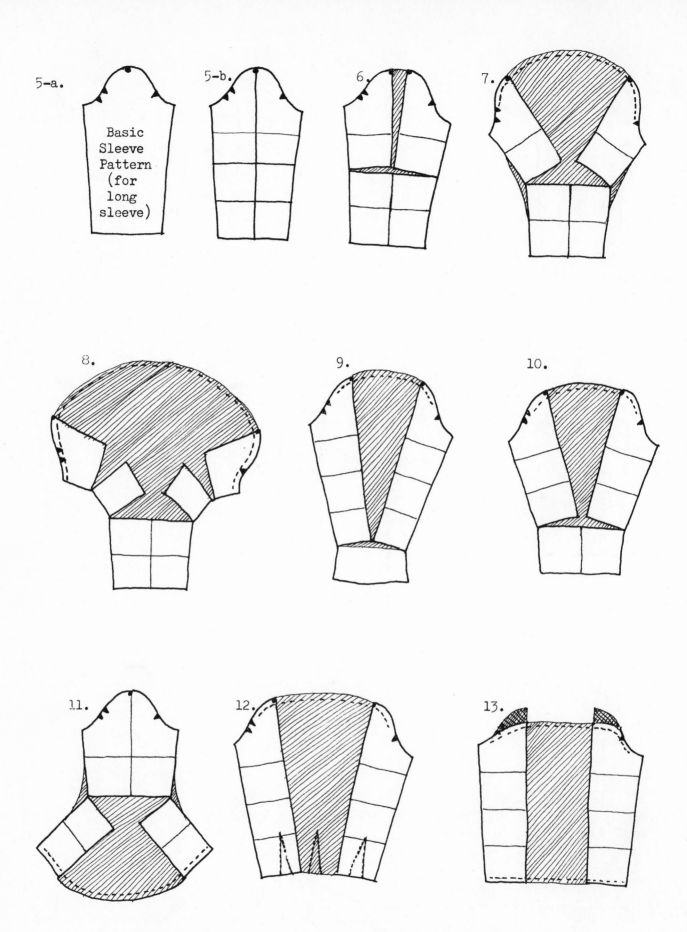

5-a.

Basic
Sleeve
Pattern
(for
long
sleeve)

5-b.

6.

7.

8.

9.

10.

11.

12.

13.

Sleeves (*continued*)

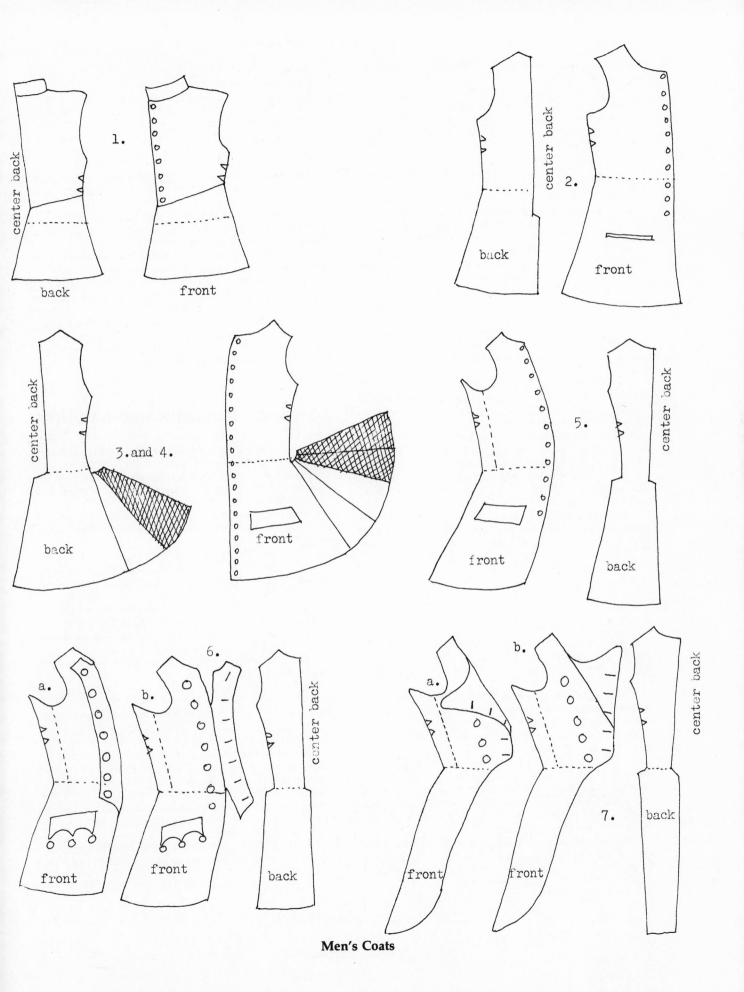

Men's Coats

period lines you want so that you can recognize similar ones when you see them.

The coat diagrams are only to give you an idea of the shape you should work for in different periods. The natural waistline is indicated by a dotted line on all the diagrams. Where there is a side back seam instead of a side seam, the place where the side would be is indicated by a dotted line also.

1. Early 17th century coats had high waists and the upper part of the armhole at the shoulder was dropped down onto the arm.

The skirt flaps and the waistline varied according to the precise period but this can help you with the general shape.

2. In mid and late 17th century, coats grew long and began to flare. This shape can usually be found in commercial patterns for women.

3. In late 17th century the coats grew quite full with pleats at the sides. Do not use the shaded section of the pattern for coats before 1700.

4. The shaded additions to the coat pattern are for the first half of the 18th century when coats reached their fullest. During mid-century they began to lose the fullness.

5. Not only did coats of the last half of the 18th century lose their skirt fullness but they began to be cut away toward the back both above and below the waist as shown. The side seam indicated by a dotted line has moved toward the back to become a side-back seam.

6. Military coats were similar in cut to fashionable coats. They usually had lapels which folded back. Officers often wore them lapped over each other in double-breasted fashion. Diagram "a" shows the lapels folded back, "b" shows the cut of the front.

7. Early 19th century coats were cut away still more below the waist while the lapels grew larger. The dotted lines indicate the natural waist and the side seam line.

Diagram "a" shows the lapels folded back, "b" shows the cut of the coat front.

HATS AND BONNETS

Hats are much easier to make than people think. You just have to think about the shape and observe the historical drawings closely. Almost any shape can be made of cardboard and cloth or felt.

Felt can be dampened and then stretched and pulled and manipulated into curved shapes. A steam iron can help in shaping felt hats, too, or reshaping old ones. You can collect old felt hats from rummage sales and reshape them into period styles.

1. The first thing to do when making a hat is to measure around the head of the person who is to wear it. Measure over the wig or hair style to be worn under it because wigs add considerably to the measurement. Add about ¾" to the measurement and cut a strip of cardboard that length to use as a guide.

2. Use your guide strip for measuring the other parts of the hat. Cut a strip of cardboard for the crown and one for the brim as shown. Draw a dot at the center of each which will be at the center front of the bonnet.

3. Cut slashes down from the top of the crown piece and in from the edge of the brim as shown.

4. By spreading these slashes apart, you can flare the pieces as much as you want while keeping the original head measurement intact.

5. For a hat like that of Figure 214 on which the crown gets smaller at the top, you can close and overlap the slashes to contract instead of expand the shape.

It is important that you keep the edge with the head measurement intact since that must remain the same as it was in the beginning.

6. When the cardboard pattern is the shape you are working for, stabilize it with masking tape or glue and paper and use that to make your final pattern.

7. When assembling the actual hat, use small cloth or paper tabs for joining the parts as shown.

8. The completed cardboard bonnet now is ready to be covered with cloth by the method demonstrated under "Covering the Cardboard Hat with Cloth."

The pattern for the hat can be used for a felt bonnet also. The felt will have to be stiffened with a commercial felt stiffener from a milliners' supply house or liquid white glue applied with a large brush.

COVERING THE CARDBOARD HAT WITH CLOTH

1. The pattern for the bonnet can be used for a bonnet of felt or of cardboard covered with cloth. If felt is used, the bonnet will need stiffening with glue, commercial felt stiffener, or by gluing two layers of felt together and letting it dry for several hours.

If you use cardboard for the bonnet, you will need to cover it with cloth. For your first bonnet it will be best to use a cotton cloth.

2. Use the bonnet brim and crown patterns (Number 1) and allow about 1" all the way around the brim as shown. Allow only ½" all the way around for the crown piece. Clip the edges as shown.

3. Cover the outside of the hat brim completely by painting on liquid white glue. Spread the glue about 1" up onto the crown. Apply the cloth quickly as shown with the clipped edges extending up on the brim.

Glue the clipped edges of the brim cover over the edge to the inside as shown.

4. Draw around the top of the crown and cut a piece of cloth 1" larger all the way around. Clip the edges. Paint the top with glue, going over the sides and spreading the glue down onto the sides for about 1". Apply the top cloth piece with clipped edges down on the sides as shown.

5. The cover for the side of the crown should be turned under so that the piece fits perfectly with no raw edges exposed. This will cover all the clipped edges and give a finished look to the outside. When you apply the glue to the crown side, be sure to cover the clipped edges of the cloth as well and cover the entire side down to where it joins the brim.

6. Cut another piece for the inside brim precisely the size of the pattern, allowing the extra inch only on the inner edge.

7. Paint the inside of the brim with glue, being care-

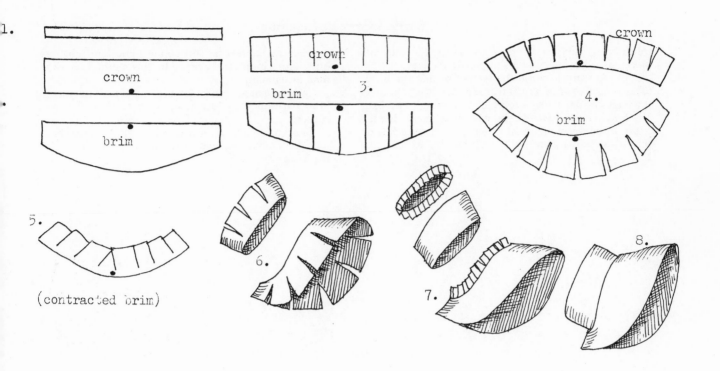

1.

crown

brim

crown

3.

brim

crown

4.

brim

5.

(contracted brim)

6.

7.

8.

COVERING THE CARDBOARD HAT WITH CLOTH

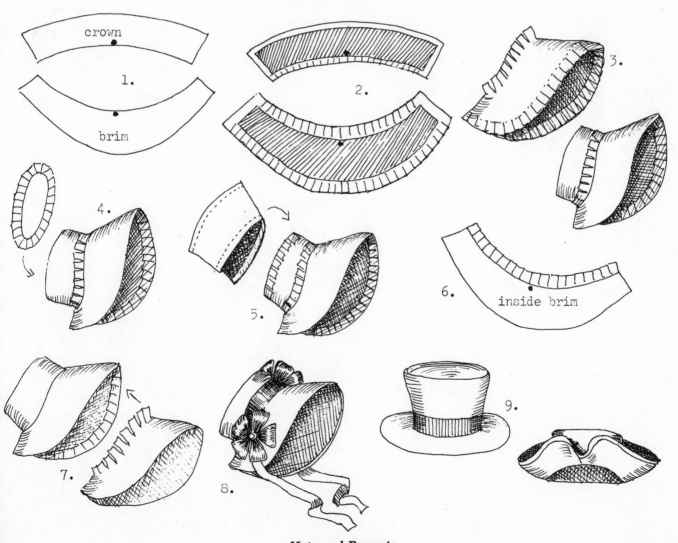

crown

1.

brim

2.

3.

4.

5.

6.

inside brim

7.

8.

9.

Hats and Bonnets

ful to bring the glue to the edges. Press the cloth into place. Glue the clipped tabs up inside the bonnet.

If you want to finish the bonnet so that the inside looks attractive, glue a ribbon around the inside to cover the edges of the cloth—even glue in a label if you like.

8. When the covered bonnet has had time to dry, it is ready to be decorated in the fashion of the early 19th century as shown here and in Figures 194, 195, 221, and 222.

9. Any hat (except soft bonnets and hats which require only cloth) can be made by this method for either man or woman.

When making a tricorne hat, make the hat with the brim flat and then turn it up later to form the three corners.

For straw hats, cover with yellow or tan cloth. Beaver hats can be covered with black velvet or silk hats with black satin.

Index

(*Note:* Page numbers in bold face refer to illustrations.)

Index

Index

Index